SOME OF THE QUESTIONS YOU'LL FIND ANSWERED IN **DIVORCED KIDS**

- What is the best way to handle the situation when my ex comes to get the kids for the weekend?
- How do I establish consistent discipline when my efforts are constantly undermined every other weekend by my ex?
- How will my children be affected by dating or remarriage? How can I help them understand and feel secure?
- What about grandparent visitation?
- Should I expect my children to help with household chores now that I have a double load, or should I protect them from added responsibilities?

You'll find practical, workable advice on these issues and more in this compassionate book.

DIVORCED KIDS

*What You Need to Know
to Help Kids
Survive a Divorce*

Laurene Johnson and Georglyn Rosenfeld

FAWCETT CREST • NEW YORK

A Fawcett Crest Book
Published by Ballantine Books
Copyright © 1990 by Laurene Johnson and Georglyn Rosenfeld

Library of Congress Catalog Card Number: 90-37931

ISBN 0-449-22076-1

This edition published by arrangement with Thomas Nelson, Inc.

Manufactured in the United States of America

First Ballantine Books Edition: July 1992

To my children, Cheri and Brad, who taught me what I needed to know to help them survive my divorce.

Laurene Johnson

To my children, Nathan and Natalie Estruth, who continue to love and forgive, and who one day soon will apply what they have learned to families of their own.

Georglyn Rosenfeld

Contents

ACKNOWLEDGMENTS *ix*
PROLOGUE *xi*

1 How Divorce Affects Children   *1*
2 Death of a Relationship   *14*
3 Mourning the Loss   *25*
4 The Road to Recovery   *37*
5 Visitation   *49*
6 Common Visitation Mistakes   *53*
7 Guidelines for Visitation   *60*
8 When a Child Has to Travel   *70*
9 Holidays   *76*
10 Between Visits   *82*
11 Communicating with a Hostile Ex-Spouse   *87*
12 Communicating with Hostile Children   *99*
13 Does Divorce Mean Discipline Problems?   *112*
14 Making Discipline More Effective   *123*
15 Protecting and Nurturing Your Child's
   Self-Esteem   *136*
16 Teaching Children to Become Self-Sufficient   *149*
17 Enlisting the Support of Others   *164*
18 The Extended Family   *172*
19 Friends to the End?   *178*
20 Teachers: Friends or Foes?   *183*
21 A Child's Perception of Dating   *191*
22 His, Hers, and Ours . . . The Stepfamily   *197*
23 Forgiveness: The Ultimate Healer   *207*

Contents

EPILOGUE   *220*
NOTES   *221*
ABOUT THE AUTHORS   *225*

Acknowledgments

I would like to thank the following people who continue to inspire me through their unconditional love are: George Addair, Bruce Bromley, Beth Clark, Janita Cooper, Wilma Hansen, Kim Johnson, Paul Kelcher, Arnold Lopez, Ken Magid, Og Mandino, Jane Monachelli, Ruth Murray, Cavett Robert, Charmaine Rusu, Jim Smoke, Diana Steffes, Denis Waitley, and Mary Ann Wall.

Laurene Johnson

Those I want to thank for their support during my divorce and their contributions to this book are:

Roger Axford, Ph.D., my professor at ASU, who walked with me during the dark days and introduced me to . . .

James Gough, M.D., who helped me survive the temporary but prolonged loss of my children;

Tom Murphy, who believed in my abilities, gave me a writing job and lots of plane tickets so I could see my kids;

Denis Waitley, Ph.D., who inspired and motivated me with his patience and friendship;

Ron Haynes, our acquisition editor, who encouraged us to write the book and made the process lots of fun;

Carol Hubbard, Eddie Parker, and Naomi Tyler, who assisted with the research;

Rob Johnson, who formulated and refined many of the concepts and ideas;

My parents, George and Nelie Gray Pannel; my brother and sister, George Pannel and Cindy Paxton; and my extended family, who continue to provide my children and me with unlimited love and support;

Bill Watkins, managing editor at Thomas Nelson, who guided the slant and direction of the book; as well as Jennifer Farrar and Wendy Peterson, who edited the manuscript;

. . . and a special word of appreciation to all the innocent victims who shared their feelings, comments, and stories with us in this book, those whose lives were emotionally shattered and forever altered by their parents' divorce, the divorced kids.

Georglyn Rosenfeld

Prologue

The world breaks everyone and afterward many are strong at the broken places.
> Ernest Hemingway
> *A Farewell to Arms*

Divorced kids come in all sizes and emotional states. Some are scarred for life, others are well adjusted. Some have good relationships with both parents, others have been abandoned. Some are still angry, others have learned to forgive their parents. Some see themselves as incapable of believing in a long-term love relationship, others are totally committed to making their marriage work so their kids will not suffer like they did.

What determines how children respond to divorce? Age and sex are a factor, but there is no "good" age for divorce. Even twins respond differently, depending upon their coping methods. For some children the greatest impact is felt two to ten years after the divorce. Far more significant than age and sex is the relationship between the parents and between the child and *both* parents before, during, and after the divorce.

Children who have the most difficult time with divorce usually come from families who have never coped well with other stressful events. Parents who only escalate the war after the divorce may as well have remained married. Parents who physically or emotionally remove themselves from a child's life make it more difficult for a child to adapt and accept the divorce.

Children who fared the best after the divorce were those who had a strong emotional center—those who felt loved, worthwhile, secure, and who learned to take responsibility for themselves and their reactions. Their emotional health stabilized them and allowed them to express anger, to grieve, and to recover emotionally from the trauma.

Unfortunately, many children do not have a healthy emotional base upon which to begin their healing. It is for these children that divorce often becomes a devastating psychological process, destined to leave permanent emotional scars. However, all children, emotionally healthy or not, will need help in handling their parents' divorce.

Parents are the first line of assistance, whether they recognize it or not. In the midst of their own grief and pain, it is often too easy for parents to deny their children's pain, but denial only compounds the problem. Parents must recognize that their children feel great pain, though they may not demonstrate it openly. A parent must strive to respect the relationship that the children have with their other parent, honor the children's desire for neutrality, and maintain positive relationships with their children as much as possible.

When we (Laurene and Georglyn) met, we were each writing a book on helping children survive divorce. Laurene worked full-time as a reality therapist, counseling hundreds of children of divorce, as well as facilitating Children Facing Divorce workshops. Georglyn worked as a free-lance writer, occasionally teaching workshops for children of divorce in local churches. Laurene asked children to draw pictures to describe divorce feelings. Georglyn used a questionnaire that the children filled out. Together we had hundreds of pictures and comments from children of all ages who were going through divorce. After comparing notes, we found a common thread running through all the children's comments—intense pain that lingers, even many years after the divorce.

Both of us were emotionally overwhelmed by the insights the children provided, especially since both of us had experienced difficult divorces. Realizing our goals and purposes were the same in our individual books, we decided to collaborate and write one book.

Throughout this book we speak with one voice unless specifically referring to Laurene's experience, as in the last chapter. It is our sincere hope that our combined experience will help you ease the strain of divorce for your children.

This book is not intended to be a psychological treatise or technical documentary of facts, figures, and graphs of the effects of divorce on children. Instead, this book looks at what determines a child's welfare during and after the divorce and helps parents, extended family, and other interested adults understand what they must do to enable children to cope with the loss and minimize the damage. Further, it shows positive steps parents can take to move themselves and their children along the road to recovery.

Our purpose is to speak for the children and help parents realize that their own reactions to the divorce frequently increase their children's pain. Throughout the book are statements children have made to us that describe the emotional impact divorce has had on their lives.

We are not social scientists or researchers who have documented every case study. However, we are two women who, in the past twelve years, have suffered through and recovered from a wide range of divorce-related traumas. Our children have also suffered, yet we feel that they emerged victorious. They have survived with high self-esteem and are responsible, well-adjusted, productive, and fully functional, though the scars of the divorce will remain forever.

Writing this book became a two-family project. Our children, all of whom are now in college or graduate school, assisted in writing and editing the book. We shared our ideas with our kids and asked, "What did we do right?" and "What did we do wrong?" Their comments were shocking, hurtful, pleasing, loving, but most of all forgiving.

We want to share our mistakes . . . which were most often a result of putting our own needs above our children's or an innocent reaction to a new situation. We also want to share our joys and victories in the hope that it will help you minimize the damage to your children (or children you care about) who will always perceive themselves as "divorced kids."

1

How Divorce Affects Children

I was real young. I didn't know what was going on. I knew Dad was missing, but I didn't know why.
Eight-year-old girl

I was very mad at my father and I wanted him to die so I could remember him the way he was before he left us, not what he had turned into.
Nine-year-old boy

My dad didn't leave us. My mom took me while I was sleeping and she left him. I didn't even know about it.
Five-year-old girl

I currently reside with my grandparents. I have lived with them since I was nine. My mom and dad have both divorced three times. I went through the first divorce and my mom's second divorce. My grandparents sheltered me from the other divorces.
Eighteen-year-old boy

If the nuclear family can be likened to a small, quiet pond, its waters unruffled and at peace, then divorce is a large boulder hurled violently into its middle. The shock

1

waves surge across the entire surface, leaving no edge untouched.

Virtually every American's life is touched by divorce . . . from the upper echelons of society to the homeless on the streets. Watching the rich and famous divorce has practically become a spectator sport in America. Unfortunately, unlike most sports, in divorce neither side wins. And worse yet, the biggest losers are the children. Divorce legally severs a marriage, but it also frequently severs the parental relationship, making the children feel that their parents not only divorced each other, but also divorced them.

Although adults experience a significant amount of trauma while going through a divorce, children not only suffer during the process but continue to suffer long after the final papers have been signed. Children of divorce battle fear and humiliation for many years, their perception of themselves drastically altered by the loss of their family. This stigma follows these children throughout their lives, making them feel like "divorced kids." Struggling to find their own way to cope with the trauma, some children strike out with behavior problems while others succumb to cripplingly low self-esteem. In their weakened emotional condition, divorced kids often blame themselves for the divorce.

No one escapes the trauma of a fragmenting family—parents, children, grandparents, and extended family are all affected.

Unfortunately, kids are often the forgotten element in a divorce. Parents are truly in the driver's seat, with access to friends, divorce recovery groups, support groups, church groups, lawyers, and counselors. Children are all too often left to fend for themselves. To an adult, a marriage—even with children—may be a relatively recent event in life's time line. To children, however, the family unit is all they have ever known. It is their world, containing their earliest and most profound memories. The split in the marriage cracks the deepest foundations of their lives, and suddenly everything is unstable. What can they depend on? Can anything be trusted?

VARIETY OF RESPONSES TO DIVORCE

There seem to be as many different reactions to divorce as there are different kinds of children. Nevertheless, most fall into several well-defined categories. And not surprisingly, the feelings children have are similar to the grieving process that adults experience during a tragedy. In addition, they suffer from a devastating loss of self-esteem, a feeling of responsibility for the divorce, and other emotions that are frightening in their intensity.

In this chapter we will attempt to grasp the enormity of this problem, using many actual comments from children of divorce and taking a look at the way children react to divorce in general. First, let's consider a sampling of the most common responses children have to divorce.

Sadness

A four-year-old girl said, "I cry at night when I'm in bed, but my mom never knows."

One twelve-year-old boy wrote, "I wouldn't miss my dad so much if I didn't hear my mom crying so hard every night. It's not fair my dad isn't here to do his job."

"It really hurt," commented a teen. "It was hard for me to accept not being able to live in the same house with both parents."

Many teenagers drew pictures of their feelings, sketching simple broken hearts and sad faces. Several drew dark clouds with a drizzling rain or eyes with tears pouring out. Others drew hearts being torn in two or stabbed.

Even children who welcomed their parents' divorce as an end to bitter fighting and distress still felt upset. "I felt glad," wrote one child, "but it was like losing a good friend too." Another said, "I felt sad at the time but realized later it was best for everyone."

No matter what other reactions children may demonstrate toward their parents' breakup, a deep, pervasive sorrow is always present. Sadness and despair can dominate their lives.

And sometimes children cling to this sadness because letting go of it feels like a betrayal. Children may feel that if they are sad for "long enough," what they had will come back; by giving up the sadness, they are giving up the chance of a happy ending, as well as betraying the object of their loss.

What children need to know is that their sadness is not a "contract" that will bring back their lost parent, home, or family structure. At the same time they need to understand that it's OK to feel sad, and they will ultimately feel happy again.

One of the best things you can do for your children is allow them to express their grief. Prolonged crying and preoccupation with the lost relationship are normal responses. They can actually help the child move through the adjustment period after the divorce. Parents who are trying to deal with their own trauma, however, may find it difficult to deal with a grief-stricken, despairing child who is acting out feelings the parents may be trying to avoid. But children need to be assured that they will not drive their parents away if they act sad or angry. Parents frequently try to hide their own grief from their children, but by expressing it in front of them, they can validate their children's pain.

Doug never saw his father express any grief or sadness over the divorce. He was always told, "Your mother was the cause of all our problems and now the cause has left. We are going through a few adjustments and some hardships, but life goes on." Although Doug felt devastated by his mother's departure, he thought, "Look how strong Dad is. I should be strong too and not feel bad about it." When Doug grew up, however, he found out from his grandparents that his father was actually severely depressed over the divorce and even contemplated suicide.

Realizing that his father's stoic attitude had all been a façade, Doug felt totally disillusioned and doubted whether his father had ever been emotionally open and aboveboard with him.

Contrast Doug's father with Jerry, a psychiatrist friend of mine, who was devastated when his wife of twenty years filed for divorce. For more than a month he had frequent crying spells, which usually occurred when he was alone. One weekend when his teenage sons were visiting, they started watching a movie that reminded Jerry of his courtship days with his estranged wife, and he was overcome with sadness. First, tears ran silently down his cheeks, then he started crying, then he sobbed uncontrollably as the memories of twenty years of happiness and love, pain and sorrow came crashing down on him. His sons had never seen their father cry. Nothing they did or said could console him. Unable to handle seeing their father lose control of his emotions, they called their mother and asked her to come pick them up.

At the time, it was a scary experience for the kids, but later they told their father that it validated their own feelings of sadness and helped them realize that it was all right to cry sometimes when they felt like it. After all, if their father, a well-known psychiatrist, cried over the divorce, it must be the mentally healthy thing to do.

It is important for all of us to know that we do not have to be sad all the time or carry our grief around forever. We will always keep our memories. And the sadness for what we have lost will always be available if we need to feel it again.

Feelings of Abandonment and Isolation

A ten-year-old boy described divorce this way: "It makes me feel like my arms and legs aren't attached."

"Daddy left. Will Mommy leave me too? What will happen to me?" an eight-year-old girl wondered.

"Even when your dad is bad," an eight-year-old boy

said, "you don't want him to leave because he's still your father."

"I thought it was my fault at first and I thought they hated me. Then they fought about custody and I thought nobody wanted me. The second and third times I was relieved about the divorce and had no negative feelings," wrote one tragic child.

Dr. Ken Magid, a psychologist, and Walt Schreibman, a marriage and family counselor in Evergreen, Colorado, collaborated in 1980 to produce a book called *Divorce Is . . . A Kid's Coloring Book*, which has proved useful to many children of divorce. All the panels contain a boy and his dog. One of them shows the pair in front of the refrigerator. On the door is a note that says, "Be back in a year or two, love Mom."[1] This fear, strongest among younger children, is quite literal. They feel they will be left to fend for themselves—after all, if one parent walked out, what's to keep the other from doing the same? Some recently divorced mothers even report that whenever they come home just five minutes late from work, they find their children hysterical.

The fear of abandonment often manifests itself as loneliness. Some of the pictures children drew for us describing divorce depict empty rooms with closed doors and windows, empty boxes and squares with nothing in the middle. One student caught the wrenching pain in a picture of a mangled dog lying in the street with tire treads over it and a car speeding away.

Children also feel abandoned when parents begin dating. A triangle of Dad, me, and his girlfriend creates much confusion. A child feels replaced by the girlfriend. Randy, an adolescent, closes the door to his room, listens to the stereo, and cuts off communication with Dad. Dad doesn't understand why Randy has stopped talking to him and says, "He's just a teenager—they're all like that." Randy experiments with new friends and drugs—he medicates himself to escape. Randy doesn't understand his feelings—he just knows he feels empty.

Confusion and Disorientation

Far and away the most common problem for children of divorce is an inability to understand what in the world has just happened to them. In their resourcefulness and intelligence, they arrive at a number of conclusions—many, unfortunately, that are wrong—in an effort to simply find answers and just try to cope.

"I really didn't understand at first," said one teen, looking back on his parents' divorce when he was five, "but as the years went by, I thought it was my fault. It was a very confusing time for me."

A nine-year-old boy remarked, "Divorce is like two lions in a den attacking each other. You know somebody is going to get hurt real bad. All kids can do is sit behind a window and watch it happen."

A group of teenagers were asked to draw pictures of what divorce felt like to them. Many of the pictures contained turbulent, chaotic scribbling—some surrounding a brain, some enveloping a heart. One picture showed an out-of-control car careening toward a tree. One teen drew a giant question mark with arrows, like turn indicators, pointing in opposite directions as if to ask, "What do I do now?"

One boy, who had experienced five separate divorces, confessed, "It was scary the first time and also confusing. The other four times it was almost like old hat."

Children's lives revolve around their family—it is all they have ever known. To hear from Mom and Dad that they will no longer be living together is more than a child can comprehend.

Feeling Torn between Parents

This is perhaps the most wrenching feeling kids have to struggle with, and many times parents do nothing but add fuel to the fire.

Pictures describing these feelings included many houses that were being cut in two . . . some even split by lightning. One picture showed four children trying to push the house back together while it was splitting down the middle. A teenager drew a circle with a jagged line down the middle, dark on one side and light on the other. Another drew two houses separated by a giant mountain range. One boy drew a picture of Washington and Arizona with himself in the middle and arrows pointing toward each state. Several kids drew pictures of themselves with outstretched arms, Mom pulling on one arm and Dad pulling on the other.

"Dad couldn't really be as bad as Mom says he is," said a nine-year-old girl.

"My mom cries when I tell her about Dad's girlfriend," one twelve-year-old said. "I can't help it if I like her just a little. She's nice to me."

"I looked at my dad's check from his boss. He makes lots of money and tells my mom he's poor. He's a liar. I can't tell him though, because he might not like me," a sixteen-year-old girl told me.

Frequently, innocent remarks by the child become a battlefield for the parents. Kids soon learn that they can no longer share things with Mom or Dad. They just get bounced back and forth between vengeful parents, and everyone ends up in trouble.

A group of children, parents, lawyers, and psychologists were asked to name events they believed had a significant negative impact on children in broken families. Some of the events included:

• When one parent tells the child that he or she doesn't like that child spending time with the other parent.
• When one parent asks the child questions about the other parent's private life.
• When one parent says bad things about the other.
• When relatives say bad things to the child about his or her parents.
• When one parent tells the child not to tell some things to the other parent.

- When parents talk to children about which parent they want to live with.
- When parents make children feel like they have to choose between Dad and Mom.

A nine-year-old boy summed it all up when he said, "I don't care who I live with, I love you both. Please don't make me choose—just tell me."

Forced Adulthood

A surprising number of the high-school students who put their feelings into artwork drew pictures of nuclear holocausts or cataclysmic storms—the end of life as they knew it. No matter how old or young the child, divorce usually means experiencing grief and emotional trauma much sooner than most children would have. Several students drew pictures depicting death or self-destruction. One drew a tree with a hangman's noose on it.

Divorce shatters the safe, secure fantasy world of childhood, and children are suddenly forced to replace a parent's missing marriage partner and provide companionship for someone much older than themselves.

"I hate it when my mom asks me how she looks," said one fifteen-year-old boy. "I don't like being put in that situation. I wish my dad were here to do it."

"My mom doesn't think she's a good cook. I don't want her to feel bad." Then this eight-year-old girl added, "So I tell her it's good, just like Daddy used to do."

The need of a parent for an adult partner is revealed in this boy's comment: "My mom acts sexy in front of me. She just needs a boyfriend."

Divorce also imposes worries and responsibilities on children that are far beyond their age.

"I always check the liquor cabinet in the morning after they've been fighting. I measure it," a little girl tragically confessed.

One insightful nine-year-old boy said, "I hate my

mom's boyfriend but I don't tell her. After all, she'll be alone someday when I'm gone, so I pretend I like him.''

Arnold Lopez, a therapist in Phoenix who specializes in codependency, says he sees major lifelong issues develop when a child is placed in a parental role after a divorce. He works with adolescents who have been placed in the surrogate parent or spouse role and later find themselves in need of therapy.

Some children of divorce, after reaching adulthood, say that they feel like they've missed out on childhood by being forced to become their parents' missing partners, which is frequently regarded as a form of codependency. The most common form is when a child becomes a "surrogate spouse."

Codependency

According to Lopez, when the other spouse is missing, the single parent's needs for love, belonging, and support are going unmet. This is why single parents tend to become emotionally enmeshed with their children. They discuss the details of financial burdens, daily exhaustion, loneliness, disappointments, anger, and depression with one of their kids. And the children begin to see themselves in the role of a spouse. Moms in particular tend to treat a son as a spouse, a confidant. And the sons, therefore, wind up feeling as if they have to fill Mom's needs. What a burden!

One boy said, "Dad left so suddenly that if I don't take care of Mom, she might leave me too." In later years children resent this role, and sometimes the resentment turns into anger in adolescence.

When discussing his resentments, a fourteen-year-old boy said, "I think I felt I had to be strong for my mom and my little sister. I had to be strong to help them through it . . . even though I was only five at the time."

All too frequently single parents have limited financial resources and a weak support system of family and friends who are willing, able, and close enough to help.

When this situation exists, the parent may end up not only being a poor parent, but may set up a situation in which the child ends up parenting the parent.

While discussing divorce, a nineteen-year-old woman remarked, ''In one day I could be a college student, my mother's therapist, my dad's escort, and my brother's mother. Small wonder I was a little ditzy that year.''[2]

When I share my concern about this with my clients, they bend their heads in shame. Most parents innocently put their child into this role. They don't knowingly set their children up for enmeshment. It's just that their needs are not being met and they don't see other choices at the time.

In his book *Bradshaw on: the Family*, author John Bradshaw says,

> Codependence is the most common family illness because it is what happens to anyone in any kind of a dysfunctional family. In every dysfunctional family, there is a primary stressor. This could be . . . Mom's hysterical control of everyone's feelings; Dad or Mom's physical or verbal violence . . . the divorce. . . . Anyone who becomes controlling in the family to the point of being experienced as a threat by the other members initiates the dysfunction. This member becomes the primary stressor. Each member of the family adapts to this stress in an attempt to control it. Each becomes outerdirected and lives adapting to the stressor for as long as the stress exists. Each becomes codependent on the stressor. . . . My belief is that codependence is the disease of today. All addictions are rooted in codependence, and codependence is a symptom of abandonment. We are codependent because we've lost our selves. . . . Codependence is at bottom a spiritual problem. It is spiritual bankruptcy.[3]

HOW LONG DOES THE EMOTIONAL TRAUMA LAST?

In our workshops, when we asked children the question, "How long did it take you to get over the divorce?" some of the responses were:

"You never get over it" (fifteen years after the divorce).

"I still haven't" (twelve years afterward).

"It's been four years but I'm still not over it."

"It took me about seven years to really get over it."

"I wasn't upset at the time. About a year later it hit and it lasted for a year."

"A few years of therapy."

"About five years."

"Four years."

"I still haven't gotten over it yet. I may never."

"I'm still trying to get over it" (ten years later).

The only "positive" response was:

"Not long. My dad was pretty mean."

Clearly, the injuries sustained in a divorce heal slowly, if ever. One of the great tragedies of divorce is that children come to assume that the whole world operates like their own. They don't feel that "living happily ever after" is possible. Many feel destined to repeat their parents' mistakes. One college student said, "To me, getting married is like walking over a mine field; you know it's going to explode . . . you just don't know when!"[4]

A young boy said, "I'll probably grow up and get married and have babies, and then I'll get a divorce. Everybody does." When asked what advice he'd like to give to his mom and dad, the eighteen-year-old previously mentioned who had survived five divorces said, "Don't get married."

Divorce may be the most catastrophic event the average American family is forced to overcome. For children, it violently interrupts the already tempestuous process of growing up. The adults involved in a pitched battle with each other have the advantage of a certain amount of control, even if it's minuscule, but children have none. This leaves the child in a wait-and-see posture, forever trying to adapt to changing conditions, torn between two parents, resiliency tested to the utmost.

Children are survivors by nature. With proper guidance their survival skills can be greatly improved. Parents are in the best position to help their children, but unfortunately, they are usually consumed by their own struggle for survival. Extended family, friends, and other interested adults can work with the parents to provide emotional support and minimize long-term damage to the child's mental health after a divorce.

2

Death of a Relationship

'In sickness and in health, till death do us part.' This traditional part of the marriage ceremony might well be changed to the following in modern America: 'In happiness and good health, till divorce do us part.'[1]

Frank D. Cox

The death of someone we love is never easy. Sometimes death comes suddenly and we find ourselves saying, "If only I had known in advance, I could have said the things I wanted to say, made amends, or told him I loved him." Those who suffer through a prolonged illness with a dying loved one often say, "If only she could have gone suddenly and not had to suffer like this, it would have been so much easier to handle."

Divorce is much like death in certain aspects. Sometimes it is quick and sudden, leaving the other spouse and children in shock. Other times the end of the relationship has been dragged out over many years. Emotions range from wishing it would end to hoping the marriage can be saved.

Six types of divorces were identified by Paul Bohannan in his book *Divorce and After*.

Emotional divorce: One or both spouses begin to withdraw emotionally from the other until there is an emotional detachment. The number of needs met outside the marriage increases.

Legal divorce: Papers are served, lawyers are involved, and the fight begins. Child custody becomes an issue.

14

Economic divorce: Property is divided. Standards of living are frequently lowered. Child support is determined.

Parental divorce: Parents are supposed to be divorcing each other, but all too frequently one or both also divorce the children. Custody and visitation are battled over. Children are caught in the crossfire.

Community divorce: At a wedding, friends and relatives of the bride typically sit on the right side of the church and those of the groom sit on the left. Unfortunately, this stance is often taken again at the time of the divorce. Friends are asked to choose sides. And families draw battle lines, refusing to cross into enemy territory even for the sake of the children.

Psychic divorce: When former spouses begin to think of themselves as separate entities instead of one, when the emotional bonds are finally broken, psychic divorce has taken place. Some people, however, are never able to completely detach themselves from a former spouse. They struggle with their individuality, finding it difficult to be their own person. If they can't attach to their former mate, they will frequently attach themselves in an unhealthy manner to one of their children or to a new love interest.[2]

Divorce is the death of a relationship, and frequently the death of many relationships . . . including parental ones. And like the reactions to death, the reactions to a divorce are extensive, chaotic, and confusing. Everyone in the family is affected, suddenly plunged into a world of emotions they may find terrifying and incomprehensible.

The pain of divorce is not a static thing; it moves through a process that is very much like what happens to us when someone we love dies. This is the grieving process, a progression of feelings and emotional states that move by stages. These stages don't happen in a straight line; we may experience them simultaneously, or move

back into one after we seem to have progressed into the
next.

Though these stages overlap each other, there are dis-
tinctions and a certain fairly predictable sequence that
should move continually toward ultimate healing. Grief
is the process by which we become whole again after a
great loss. It is painful, difficult, and inevitable, but the
end result is sanity and growth.

It may seem strange that a divorce provokes the same
reactions as a death, but they are very similar. Both involve the loss of a primary person and relationship, the
disruption of a family. In many ways, divorce may be
harder to cope with than death, because there is no obvious
closure—the lost person is still living, still interacting
with us.

It is important to understand that both adults and children move through these stages at different rates. For
instance, the person who decides to leave the marriage
may already have gone through some or all stages of
grieving before broaching the subject of divorce. He or
she may already have spent time denying that there were
problems in the relationship or being angry when the realization came that the relationship was not going to
work. He or she may have made bargaining attempts—to
get counseling, or to be nicer to the spouse—and when
this didn't work, depression or guilt may have been the
result. By the time the divorce happens, this partner may
have moved all the way into acceptance, while the other
partner is just entering shock.

In any divorce, the partner who leaves and the partner
who is left will be on different grief timetables. The one
left tends to go through excruciating pain, even if the
marriage had not been happy. Not only is there the loss
of the relationship to deal with, but there is also rejection
and abandonment. The one who leaves doesn't experience these feelings to the same extent.

Whether or not the adults were emotionally prepared
for it, they have usually known for some time that a di-

vorce was probably coming. Children, however, are almost always taken off guard. According to one study, 80 percent of the children were completely unprepared for their parents' divorce.[3] Often, one parent simply disappeared while the child was sleeping, or the sleeping child was removed from the home by a parent.

To compound the pain, children in a divorce tend to identify with the partner who has been left. There is additional fear, loneliness, and sadness in being the one "abandoned"; therefore, children heal more slowly, and need a great deal of support to identify and express their feelings. It's helpful for everyone involved in a divorce to remember that grief is temporary. Children fear that it will never go away, so they need extra reassurance—as well as help to ensure—that it will in time; though there are many indications that, for children of divorce, some pain will continue to last a lifetime.

If the divorce is the first really bad thing that has ever happened to a child, he or she may have nothing to compare it with to see that it's possible to get over it. I have actually drawn out the stages of grief for children to show them how it works and explained that it will take between two and five years to work through. Children often become encouraged when they know that this is a process other people have gone through, that it is only temporary, and that the intense pain will mellow and lessen with time.

Let's take a brief look at some of the stages of grief.

SHOCK

The first reaction to hearing about any traumatic event is *shock*—an inability, rather than an unwillingness, to believe. The body sends out all the alarm signals: adrenaline shooting through the body, heart pounding . . . but the mind remains a blank. This is a merciful human response that keeps a person from being overwhelmed. Most traumatic information is absorbed slowly, requiring weeks, months, even years, to sink in.

"Come right home after school," Jim told his sons as they went out the door, "I have something to tell you." Michael and Jason, ages seven and nine, allowed their imaginations to run wild, but finally decided their dad was either going to take them on the promised trip to Disneyland or tell them they were getting a swimming pool. Their mom, Doris, had been in a wheelchair since she was twelve years old, and her doctors had suggested that a swimming pool at home would help with her therapy. Running in the door breathlessly, Michael shouted, "Dad, are we finally getting a swim. . . ."

In midsentence Michael realized his mother was crying and his father was standing by three suitcases and some shipping boxes. Dad had a hard, cold look on his face they had never seen before.

"What's going on?" Jason asked hesitantly.

"We're getting a divorce. I'm leaving and moving out of state," their father said matter-of-factly.

"No!" Jason screamed.

"What about us?" Michael asked, as he started crying.

"Your mother will take care of you. I'm leaving."

"But Mom can't take care of herself or us without you," Jason said.

Doris sat in stunned disbelief. Her mind would not allow her to accept that Jim, who had befriended her and taken care of her since she was twelve years old, could desert her and the boys. Never once had they discussed divorce. Survival was not possible without Jim.

Within fifteen minutes Jim was gone. No arguments or discussions, no hint of doom. Doris and the children stumbled through the next few weeks as if in a daze . . . unable to think, unable to feel, unable to grasp what had happened to their lives.

DENIAL

As an early stage of grieving, denial is another merciful protective mechanism. It shields us from the pain, distancing us from it with thoughts like, "This can't be happening to me," or "It can't be true," or "This kind of thing only happens to other people, not me." You will feel disoriented and confused, needing to have things explained again and again, even after you thought you understood.

In most divorces, however, denial doesn't last more than a few months. Reality makes itself known . . . in the strangeness of a new home, the cold aloneness of your bed.

Many children at this stage feel sure their parents will get back together because the harsh truth is too painful to accept. One child's denial surfaced in this statement: "My parents aren't really getting a divorce. They just aren't going to be married any more." Another said, "Divorce—you mean the 'D' word. I don't want to talk about it."

Some children whose parents have remarried and even have new children in the family still do not accept the divorce, insisting that their parents will get back together.

This is a different kind of denial, a long-term unwillingness to accept what has happened. An adult or child who takes years to come to terms with a divorce may be denying not only the situation, but the emotions that go along with it, because these feelings are so frightening and painful.

ANGER

Anger has its roots in the most positive of impulses: that of self-preservation. It is a basic reaction to an assault against oneself, a feeling that you are important and have the right to defend yourself against attack. In a divorce, anger comes out of the feeling that something you possessed has been taken away, that you have been robbed of something rightfully yours—a relationship, a way of life, a family. And since many people evaluate their lives by the things they own, they can become enraged when everything is suddenly cut in half or taken away during divorce.

Although anger can be devastating at times, it can also be a valuable defense mechanism when used constructively to head off a disaster. It *always* demands release in some way.

Children, however, rarely know how to vent their fury. They are asked to be calm and understanding while life as they've known it is dissolving. Sometimes their anger spurs them into action, as they try to repair the rift in their family before it's too late. Sometimes, they just want to explode.

Many teens who drew their responses to divorce pictured dark, brooding storms, often with lightning and thunder. One drew a burst of stars like an explosion, and another drew a machine gun firing off an angry round.

When asked to write down what divorce felt like, one eight-year-old boy aimed his fury at the furniture: "I hate my sofa. It's orange and black. It's where my parents told me they were getting a divorce. I'll never sit on it again." Other kids answered more briefly. "Anger," jotted one. "Anger, hurt, confused," wrote another.

In his book, *The Boys' and Girls' Book About Divorce*, Dr. Richard A. Gardner describes anger as "the feeling that comes out when we want something that we cannot have or which we think we cannot have."[4] Gardner goes on to give examples of anger expressed in a healthy way, such as when a child's toy is stolen and the angry reaction restores it; and times when anger is useless, such as when the toy thief is much bigger than the rightful owner. Says Gardner:

Most children of divorced parents are angry because they want their parents to get married again, and they won't. The parents say that they were divorced because they no longer loved each other and were unhappy together, and therefore they will not marry again. Such children will be angry as long as they keep hoping that their parents will change their minds. They don't stop hoping and trying, and as long as they do this, they'll be angry.[5]

Divorce gives us lots of people to be angry at—not just the partner who left or "caused" us to leave, but the world for promising happily-ever-after endings and not delivering.

Anger can be a very positive step because it shows that some acceptance has taken place, that we're getting past denial, and that we are making a protest against being hurt. During the anger stage, however, life may seem out of control, filled with emotions of frightening intensity. "I never got angry in my life, and all of a sudden I am feeling this rage within me." But take heart, this really is a sign that the healing process has begun.

People who have never shown or expressed real anger in their lives before, though, need to exercise caution with this powerful feeling.

On the other extreme, however, anger can be masked as fear or sadness when it is felt to be unacceptable. Many who would try to comfort you may be uncomfortable with anger themselves and tell you, "Calm down, you're getting hysterical," or "You're being unreasonable . . . crazy . . . childish . . ." It is important to find people who can handle your anger and listen in a nonjudgmental way. Anger that is expressed will probably be gone fairly quickly. Anger that is internalized can remain for many years, becoming increasingly self-destructive with time.

Children may have no models on which to pattern their expressions of anger, and no words to describe what they are feeling. They may act out anger in many ways—by having discipline problems, talking back to parents and teachers, or kicking the dog. Some children may become belligerent and aggressive, even violent; others may use passive-aggressive tactics, finding ways to sabotage themselves or others.

One of my clients was a twelve-year-old boy who became obsessed with knives after his parents divorced. He exhibited a lot of aggression toward his mother with the knives, even though he was actually angry at his father for leaving. This is a serious but not uncommon response to divorce. When I asked high school students to draw a picture describing how they felt about divorce, several of them drew knives, guns, or other instruments of violence. One drew a picture of a heart with a knife plunged deep into it, drops of blood dripping out of the heart.

Many children also have nightmares when they are going through divorce: dreams of violence, knives, poison, fierce animals, of their parents being eaten up by people.

One ten-year-old girl said, "I'm always dreaming of my parents dying. They drink poison and scream for help. I can't get through the door to help them. It's my fault they die. I want to take poison and die too."

Faced with this mixture of fear and anger, children need the difference between real and pretend explained to them. It is also very important that they have access to acceptable ways to vent their anger, that they understand "it is OK to hit your pillow, but it is not OK to hit your brother." Children need to know when and how they may express their anger, and they also need to know that their feelings are normal and will pass.

Adults, as well as children, need to find acceptable ways to express anger. Debbie and Tom had been married fifteen years and had six children when she discovered he was having an affair with his secretary, Celeste. After she gave him the ultimatum of getting rid of Celeste or leaving, Debbie was served with divorce papers on a Thursday while Tom was out of town. As an attorney, Tom could employ every possible legal maneuver against Debbie, but he underestimated her wrath.

Tom's prized possessions were his many tailored Italian suits, silk dress shirts gathered from around the world, expensive alligator shoes, and his antique gun collection worth over fifty thousand dollars—which was given to him by his father.

Debbie called the newspaper and ran an ad for a garage sale on Saturday:

Must sacrifice custom-made men's suits, silk shirts, expensive shoes, and antique gun collection. No item over $10.

By noon on Saturday Debbie had sold all of Tom's treasured possessions for a fraction of their worth. Then she packed up all his underwear, socks, high school and college memorabilia, trophies, books, and all his other valued possessions and dumped them in various Goodwill and Salvation Army collection bins in a town twenty miles away.

Tom came home on Monday with the intention of packing a few things and moving in with Celeste. Tom knocked on Celeste's door in a state of shock and with a new appreciation for an old phrase about the fury of a woman scorned.

Although we don't endorse Debbie's actions, getting the anger out is a positive step. If anger is not dealt with, it can result in a person becoming angry throughout his or her entire adult life. You may have run into a few of these people in your lifetime. They are brimming with hostility and anger all the time, with no apparent cause.

On the other hand, just as with sadness, people who learn to identify and express these angry feelings also learn that anger can be powerful in a positive way. The child learns that he or she has the right to get angry, to expect people to listen, and the power to object when feeling threatened. A child who is allowed to express anger can also be less prone to depression, less likely to turn the anger inward.

During this stage of grieving it is important to identify and express anger, but at some point we need to let it go. This can seem threatening if we feel that anger is our only way of having personal power: we feel that by letting it go, we may be setting ourselves up to be victims. We can release anger without releasing the power it has given us. One way of doing this is by verbalizing it: "I own my anger, and I realize it has been a positive and necessary force at this time in my life. I can identify and use anger any time I need it, so I can also let it go. I release this anger now so that I can go on with the healing process in my life."

3

Mourning the Loss

> Divorce is an easy escape, many think. But in counseling many divorcées, I have discovered that the guilt and loneliness they experience can be even more tragic than living with their problem.[1]
>
> Billy Graham

Emotions of loss are varied and complex. No two people experience divorce alike. However, many of the feelings of loss in a divorce are similar to the confusion and disorientation associated with any kind of loss. According to Frank D. Cox, author of *Human Intimacy . . . Marriage, the Family, and Its Meaning*, these emotions include a mixture of the following:

Self-pity: Why did this happen to me?

Vengeance: I'm going to get even!

Despair: I feel like going to sleep and never waking up again.

Wounded pride: I'm not as great as I thought I was.

Anguish: I don't know how I can hurt so much.

Guilt: I'm really to blame for everything.

Loneliness: Why don't our friends ever call me?

Fear: No one else will want to marry me.

Distrust: He (or she) is probably conniving with attorneys to take all the property.

Withdrawal: I don't feel like seeing anyone.

Relief: Well, at least it's over, a decision has finally been made.

Loss of feelings of psychological well-being: I feel awful, depressed, nervous, suicidal.[2]

All of these emotions are perfectly normal. As you go through a divorce, you are likely to feel almost all of them at one time or another. But somehow you must go on. You must grieve for what you have lost and look forward to what you will gain from the experience. Let's look at some more stages of grief.

BARGAINING

Bargaining is the stage at which we try to change the situation back to the way it was or to the way we want it to be. The reasoning behind it is that we can change other people's behavior by changing our own.

An adult may say, "I'll be a better husband/wife if you'll come back," or even, "If I get a new job (or lose weight, go through drug rehabilitation, or whatever), my spouse will come back."

Darla treated her husband, Raymond, like dirt, publicly degrading him, openly running around on him, and screaming at him and the children on a daily basis. She thought he would never leave her because of the children. One day Raymond had enough, however, and he left her. Even though Darla knew she treated him poorly, she wrote him letter after letter begging him to return. She promised to try to change her behavior and assured him they could work things out for the children's sake.

Raymond knew from living with her for twelve years that she really wouldn't change, and he wanted more out of life. Once Darla found out he wasn't coming back, her bargaining attempts turned to anger, and she began striking out at him in a vicious manner.

Children often try to bargain with their parents or with God to get the parents back together, promising to be good, to do all the household chores, to never ask for anything again. One child wrote: "When my dad told us he was leaving, I made him chocolate chip cookies—his favorite—and he still left us. My sister and I had a picture of us taken so he wouldn't forget us.''

Bargaining is an example of "magical thinking," a type of thinking that begins in early childhood. When we are young we see everything in relation to ourselves and conclude that we are the center of the universe. We even believe that we can cause events to happen by wanting them or thinking about them. But bargaining is not limited to childhood. Adults often fall into the "magical thinking" trap too. The problem is that the issues in a divorce cannot be wished away. The principles of bargaining are sure to create destructive illusions and ultimately lead to failure.

This stage usually doesn't last long because it quickly leads to frustration.

FEAR

Another emotion experienced in divorce is fear. Even before a marriage ends, both adults and children will probably experience the terror that comes when they realize a primary relationship may end. Children will be scared when they hear their parents fighting, and adults will probably be equally frightened of losing their spouse or by the idea of leaving the marriage. Once the marriage ends, both partners will probably be afraid of being alone, of the risk-taking required by the future. Old fears, too, of being unlovable or a failure, may surface and be exaggerated during this time.

Children, especially very young ones, tend to experience a different kind of fear: the fear that their world is no longer safe. Initially, the idea that a parent could leave the family may seem unimaginable to them; and when it happens, they may feel that other inconceivable disasters could happen to them at any time. Children also tend to have very practical fears about who is going to take care of them, like who will drive them to school, or make their lunch. Abandonment is the ultimate fear of many children, and divorce can make it seem very real. Children need to be reassured that their parents are divorcing each other but not them. Children cannot be divorced, but many end up feeling that way.

Both adults and children experience fear of the future. To a child, the future can be a nightmarish prospect. Already struggling with feelings of abandonment and isolation, many children fear they will no longer be taken care of or loved. One teenager drew a giant question mark with a death mask, as if to ask, "What is there to live for now? What can I expect?"

In about 90 percent of divorces the mother retains custody of the children and the father moves out. Sometimes the children are able to stay in the family home, but other times it must be sold and the mother and children must move to a less expensive dwelling and unfamiliar surroundings. Mom may start working outside the home for the first time and not be there as often for the children.

Many kids wonder if they are going to have to move to another city, away from friends, school, grandparents, and even their dog. The older a child is during the divorce, the more practical are the fears. Rather than worrying about being fed or having a place to sleep, they wonder if they'll ever get that first car, date money, or the chance to go to college.

A surprising number of teenagers answered the question "What did you need when your parents got divorced?" with comments relating to money. One student drew a heart with a dollar sign in the middle of it and wrote: "Money for help to forget, love to replace what is missing." Another student drew a one hundred dollar bill and put his own picture in the place of Jackson's. Other pictures showed:

- An outstretched hand with a smiley face on the palm and dollar signs at the end of each finger and thumb.
- A full page of dollar signs, many made by punching the pencil through the paper for the design.

• A large dollar bill, a house, a four-wheeler, a motorcycle, and a heart with an arrow through it.

These kids also expressed uncertainty about their own future marriage relationships and a reluctance to get involved lest they put their own children through a divorce. A nineteen-year-old girl whose parents divorced during her second year in college was devastated by the experience and immediately broke off her own engagement. "All these years I thought my parents loved each other, now I don't know if I will ever be able to believe in a lasting relationship."

GUILT

Even though it seems ludicrous, it is amazing and tragic to see the extent to which children—particularly young children—feel that they are the cause of a divorce because of some cruel thought or word they once directed at their parents. Children sometimes assume that, because they have misbehaved, they have caused the family to break up. Sometimes they go so far as to think they are bad or unlovable people. The following are actual quotes from children:

> My dad left because I wanted to ride my bike my way, and I told him to go away. He did and divorced my mom.

> If I had watched my baby brother when my mom was cooking dinner, then my mom wouldn't have left my dad. It's all my fault.

In the middle of the coloring book *Divorce Is . . . ,* by Magid and Schreibman, there are two opposing pictures. On the left we see the boy and his dog staring disconsolately at a flower pot they have just broken, with the caption, "Sometimes I think that if I had behaved better, Mom and Dad wouldn't have separated.'' On the right we see the same pair, both with wings and halos, and the caption reads: ''But Mom and Dad told me that even if kids were perfect angels parents would still get divorced, because divorce is an adult problem.''[3]

It seems that children who have the misfortune of experiencing multiple divorces learn not to take so much responsibility. One child wrote, ''I thought it was my fault at first, and I thought they hated me. Then they fought about custody, and I thought nobody wanted me. The second and third times I was relieved about the divorce and had no bad feelings.''

Children especially have no easy way to gauge how much control they have in their lives and over the choices and behavior of others. Children who believe they have caused a divorce may suffer enormous amounts of guilt secretly, since to admit the guilt would be to invite punishment or further abandonment. They may conclude that they have caused the divorce by having ''bad'' or ''wrong'' feelings, such as anger. Since divorce tends to produce more anger, children often get caught in a cycle of guilt and suppressed feelings.

However, this kind of guilt is not limited to children. Because divorce is such a complex and overwhelming situation, even adults are susceptible to blaming themselves and explaining the divorce as something specific that they can change: the divorce happened because I was a bad cook, a bad lover, or I watched too much TV—all things that can be changed in order to bring the lost partner back.

It is very important for parents to not only explain the real causes of the divorce to their children, but to ask them, either directly or indirectly, whether they feel responsible. Parents need to make sure their children understand that we do not cause others to act in certain ways by our thoughts or behavior; people always choose their own behavior.

LONELINESS

Loneliness will be felt by everyone involved in a divorce, but particularly by the partner and the children who are left. Family strength is diminished by the absence of one partner, and emotional resources are also less available because each member of the family is in pain. A seventeen-year-old girl told me, "We are half a family—lonely." When asked to draw a picture expressing her feelings about divorce, a high school girl drew an empty room with a window in it and put the word *loneliness* at the bottom.

The practical, day-to-day changes as a result of the divorce also increase loneliness. A single parent is forced to take on the responsibilities of the absent partner, sometimes working more than before for the lost wage-earner.

Latchkey children, children who are alone in the house while their parents work, are particularly susceptible to loneliness. According to one study, one in six children lives in a single-parent household, one in three will live with a single parent before age eighteen, and more than a third of all elementary students are latchkey children.[4] And loneliness will become a regular part of all these children's lives.

This emotion is difficult because it makes us feel not only alone, but alienated from the rest of the world—as though we are unacceptable, unworthy to be with others, different, isolated. It hinders us from reaching out to someone else. To say, "I'm lonely," may feel like we are admitting, "I'm no good." Loneliness can also be a vicious cycle, because when we are alone, all the painful feelings that we may have been avoiding become inescapable, furthering our sense of alienation. If being alone makes us feel guilty, scared, angry, or sad, it is easy to conclude that we are bad, no fun to be around, or crazy.

Loneliness is also felt by the non-custodial parent who is now out of his or her home and without children and spouse. When the children visit and leave, the loneliness can become more pronounced, unless he or she has a significant relationship with someone else to fall back on for support. The custodial parent may also be extremely lonely and remorseful when the children are away visiting because he or she might still want to be with the children and the ex-spouse.

And holidays are especially painful for whichever parent is without the children. They bring their own memories, for parents and children, of happier times when they were together for special family times.

Loneliness can be eased if we realize that it is a universal feeling, and that by telling someone, "I'm lonely," we are not admitting to being unlovable or weak. If the feelings we have are faced and supported rather than avoided, being alone may become less frightening. Children and adults can find satisfaction in being alone, in being self-sufficient, and having the freedom and time to think their own thoughts and understand their own feelings.

DEPRESSION

Depression has been described as anger turned inward, or anger turned inside out, but it is also a time when feelings are overwhelming and the self withdraws. Symptoms of depression include lethargy, fatigue, general melancholy, and weepiness. There may also be a weight loss or gain.

Every divorce involves depression, even after we think we have "worked through" the divorce. Although depression can be painful and frightening, it means that healing is within reach.

Care should be taken at this stage to make sure the healing occurs. If you are unable to move out of this stage, please seek professional help. Counselors, psychologists, and psychiatrists see depressed patients every day and can diagnose the severity of it much better than you can yourself. And sometimes it can be caused by a chemical imbalance, which can most likely be treated with medications. Untreated, depression can result in tragedies.

Ruth was so depressed over her divorce that nothing could comfort her. Although she told several people she felt like killing herself, they thought it was an exaggeration of her feelings. But one day, while her three children were at school, she did commit suicide. She left behind a farewell note to her children that contained strong recriminations toward her ex-husband, blaming him for her situation. Her other farewell gifts to her children were confusion, feelings of hopelessness, and depression that lasted for many years.

Feelings of helplessness and low self-esteem characterize depression. At this stage we tend to see ourselves as victims. Just as we felt an unrealistic sense of control in the bargaining stage, during depression we see ourselves as completely lacking control. When your ex-spouse remarries, you may be thrown into a deeper depression because you realize there really is no way to change your life back to the way it was. Most people need this time of withdrawal in order to assimilate all these changes in their lives. Depression gives us this time, allowing us to integrate all the feelings we have had during the grieving process so that we may go on as whole people.

The negative side of depression is that the feelings of helplessness it produces may extend to our self-image; we may begin to get stuck in the role of victim or perceive our situation as totally hopeless or helpless. Distorted thinking begins to run in a cycle: helpless thoughts make it difficult to act, our behavior becomes paralyzed, which in turn leads to more helpless thoughts. Many people need help in this stage to become "unstuck" and to see that many of their thought patterns are self-defeating and changeable. Once we realize that we have power over our thoughts, we can begin to change our negative patterns.

This may be the hardest stage to move beyond because it involves getting back into life, which requires risk-taking. It is important for us to tell ourselves, "I have been depressed for awhile and that's OK. I needed time to rest and withdraw, and it has helped me to heal. But now I am going to let go of depression and find out what I want my life to be like from now on. I deserve a good life, and I am going to work to have one."

Depression is also the stage where the most spiritual growth can occur. Maybe you drank your way through the divorce or became promiscuous to numb the pain. Neither of those worked, so now you are willing to try God. When we are as far down as we can go, we look at our lives and say, "I denied it, I became angry about it, I tried to get it back together again, but it is not going to happen. So what is going to happen to me?" Depression shows we are beginning to come to terms with the divorce, that we have finally come to an understanding of what has happened. It is at this stage that we become ready to truly move forward and heal ourselves.

ACCEPTANCE

Probably the most tragic divorce situation described in this book is the case of Doris and Jim, whose situation was detailed in the last chapter in the section on shock.

Crippled, with no medical insurance, unable to drive, never having worked, no marketable skills, and two young boys to care for, Doris was left to survive with only a meager amount of child support. Although getting through each stage of the grieving process was a struggle, she managed to survive. Her children also survived.

Church friends rallied around her and created a new life for her. They arranged for Doris to take correspondence courses and other classes through educational TV. They drove her where she needed to go. And her single friends raised money to buy her a car with hand controls so she was able to learn to drive. Her boys were soon strong enough to carry her places where she could not go in a wheelchair. When someone loaned her a computer, Doris learned several software programs and became quite proficient at them. Eventually she found a job doing computer work at home and became financially self-sufficient.

With her newly developed skills and the love and support of her friends, she moved through the grieving process and into acceptance, able to help her children do the same, even though their father still hasn't contacted them in the twelve years since he left. (If he were available for an interview, he would probably be a classic case study in guilt.)

Michael and Jason, their children, also gradually moved into acceptance. After a year of no response to their numerous letters asking him to come home and no phone call from their father, Michael and Jason realized their father probably didn't intend to ever contact them again.

Rather than running home to check the mailbox every day, they began to tell their mother, "Just think of all the things Dad is missing: he won't get to see me pitch in the championship Little League game—you know how he always loved my games. . . ."

"I bet Dad is really sorry he missed my eighth-grade graduation."

"You know Mom, even though it's been hard on you, you are the lucky one. You get to spend time with us every day, see us grow up, graduate from high school, go to college, get married, and have kids. Dad is going to miss all of that. He won't even get to know about all the great things that are going to happen in our lives."

Gradually, they began to feel sorry for their father rather than for themselves. Going through the grieving stages and accepting the inevitable closely coincided with Doris's adaptation to her situation and determination to survive.

When we reach the point of acceptance, our lives and

our selves are becoming whole again. Acceptance means that we fully understand what we have lost, yet we are able to see the emotional and spiritual growth we have gained. Painful feelings have been worked through, and we can say, "Yes, this has hurt, but I'm going to make it; and not only am I going to make it, I am going to enjoy my life even more than before because of all the things I have learned."

our selves are becoming whole again. Accept the events

4

The Road to Recovery

From what you see on TV and in the movies, you'd think that getting a divorce was some yellow brick road to personal growth and happiness. . . . But ask someone who's been through it. There is nothing funny or easy about divorce. It is a savage emotional journey. Where it ends, you don't know for a long time.[1]

Abigail Trafford

Divorce is first and foremost a crisis. When we are in a crisis, we are locked into the present, the past slips away, taking all our security with it, and the future seems non-existent. The present holds pain, pain that must be experienced and dealt with, or it will go on and on without stopping.

Trina Bertiger, a Mesa, Arizona, psychotherapist, says, "The worst experience in the world is a messy divorce. An unmessy divorce, if there is such a thing, is probably the second worst thing . . . Divorce is a loss of a relationship, a difficult procedure, even if you want it. . . . A divorce is painful because it's a change, a major transition in life, and changes are never easy."

Divorce is both a process and a journey. Many times you might feel that you are not moving forward at all, but stumbling helplessly backward. We want to encourage you, that even though it may feel this way, you *are* moving forward, going through the process of healing. Every experience, event, feeling, and thought you have is one step closer to healing and wholeness. Remember that nothing is in vain, not even a marriage that didn't last. You are the sum total of your life experiences, and this is one of those influential experiences that will help you grow exponentially.

Divorce, whether we like it or not, is going to change our lives. When we have moved through it, we will be different. This does not mean we will never feel the pain again; the experiences and the feelings that went with the divorce will always be part of our lives. Your children's ability to adapt to the divorce is going to depend on your ability to adapt to the divorce. If you carry negative feelings and emotions, they will also. The sooner you begin to heal, the sooner your children will start on their road to recovery.

One technique for having a more successful life after a divorce is called *dumping the garbage*. The Reverend Thomas O'Dea of the Holy Spirit Parish in Tempe, Arizona, created this acronym.

Garbage can be seen as:

G—Guilt
A—Anger
R—Resentment
B—Bitterness
A—Anxiety
G—Greed
E—Envy

Mary Ann Wall, a reality therapist in Phoenix, Arizona, told me,

Garbage is all the negative things that infect adults' and children's lives. Garbage inhibits our ability to effectively meet our basic needs. Garbage blocks our potential. It clogs up our effective living. If we are going to be free, we must let go of the garbage. When we have garbage in our house, we put it in a bag and throw it away. We don't decorate it.

An example of decorating emotional garbage is saying, "I have a right to be angry. Look at what he has done to me," or, "I'll make her pay dearly."

Author Richard Flint offers advice on what to do with the garbage in our lives, "Each of us lives with a trash can on the inside of us. Each day we dump into the can. The problem with many is they have not learned there is a trash pick-up every day. We are the most dangerous when we are not dumping our can on a daily basis."[2]

So how do we dump the garbage?

GARBAGE DUMPING EXERCISES

Letter exercise.

Write a letter to your ex-spouse. Say exactly what you feel . . . all the nasty, dirty, mean thoughts you have ever had, and then tear it up and have a burning ceremony.

"Stop, erase, replace" exercise.

Picture a blackboard. Now picture a negative thought on that blackboard represented by a dirty line that has made a smudge. Now say the word *stop*. Picture yourself erasing the dirty smudge, the negative thought. After you erase the mark, picture yourself taking a red marker and drawing over it a beautiful, loving heart. What you are actually doing with this exercise is stopping the negative thoughts, erasing them, and replacing them with a beautiful thought. Use something that reminds you of beauty and love, something good and positive and beautiful.

Bag exercise.

Write out your negative thoughts and put each one on a separate sheet of paper. Then wad them up and put them in a bag; then literally walk them out to the garbage. This sounds a little funny, but it works.

Shower exercise.

Walk into the shower, turn on the water, and visualize all the negative feelings you have ever had about your ex-spouse and the divorce washing off your body and going down the drain. While you are getting the outside of your body clean, you get the inside clean too.

Pollution exercise.

Think of yourself as a stream; if a stream is clear, the water flows. If it has garbage or pollution in it, it doesn't flow straight or pure. Negative thoughts and actions cause pollution in otherwise clear water. The Environmental Protection Agency (EPA) fines companies for polluting the environment and sometimes makes them assist in the cleanup operations. Be your own EPA. Be on guard for negative thoughts that are polluting your mind. Rather than fining yourself, reward yourself for cleaning up your own stream of consciousness.

Journal exercise.

Each day write all your negative and positive feelings in a notebook. Keep writing in it for several months until you notice you are recording more positive feelings than negative feelings. Save your journals. Occasionally read them over when you are having a tough time handling the divorce. Several clients began writing poetry again for the first time in years.

Family history exercise.

Write the story of your family's history. Begin with the day you met your spouse, telling about your courtship and wedding ceremony. Be sure to include the happy times as well as the sad times. Write about the birth and childhood experiences of each child. Describe the fights and difficulties. Record what you believe to be the cause of the divorce. Describe how much you love each child. Write several alternative happy endings to your story or leave the pages blank. If you like, add some pictures from your family album. Show the book to your children if they are old enough to understand. If not, create a separate storybook for each child that you can read to them or that they can read for themselves to help maintain their family identity and try to understand what happened. Don't overlook the importance of this for your children. If your version is too negative, write and illustrate a separate one for the children. Do not place the blame for the divorce on the other person. Reinforce the love you and your ex-spouse have for them, even though you don't love each other anymore or aren't going to be married.

"Light at the end of the tunnel" exercise.

Right now you might feel that, emotionally, you are in a long, dark tunnel in the deepest recesses of the earth . . . and may never find your way out. Think about that tiny point of light you see in the far distance ahead of you. What is that light? Think about what you want to see when you get closer to the end of the tunnel. Remember, you are moving forward, not going backwards. What would you like for your life to be like? Write it down and think about it in some of your dark moments. If necessary, think of yourself as a train zooming down the track, obliterating everything and everybody that stands in the way of your healing.

"Goals and purpose" exercise.

Sit down and have a planning session with yourself. Identify what you believe to be your life's purpose. Make a list of what you would like to accomplish in the next five years. (Avoid writing down a goal of destroying your ex-spouse's present and future love relationship or preventing him or her from seeing the children.) Write down goals for all areas of your life—physical, mental, emotional, spiritual, recreational, vocational, etc. Make specific goals for what you want to accomplish in relation to the divorce, custody, and visitation. Remember to put the best interests of your children above any desire for revenge. Work on your list for several days or weeks. Dream. Plan. Evaluate. *Begin*.

Exercise exercise.

Increase the amount of time you exercise each day. If you don't exercise at all, start taking a twenty-minute walk each day. (When hostilities are high, write your ex-spouse's name on the bottom of your tennis shoes or put his or her picture in your shoe and stomp on it for twenty minutes while you exercise.) Gradually increase your walks to longer lengths of time, or walk more than once a day. If you are in good physical health, begin a more rigorous routine. Work in a game of tennis at least once a week. Take a bike ride with your kids or a friend. Jog. Swim. Jump on a minitrampoline. Run up and down the stairs in your home or at work.

Cemetery exercise.

Go for a long walk in a cemetery. Feel the peace and quiet. Look at the tombstones. Read the epitaphs. Notice how old the people were when they died and how long ago they were buried. Observe the number of family members buried next to each other . . . husbands and wives who have one headstone. Think about how you would like your epitaph to read. How would you like your ex-spouse's epitaph to read?

Now go to the children's section of the cemetery. Look at the ages of the children who are buried there. See if any families have more than one child buried next to each other.

Count your blessings. Realize you may have lost custody of your children or have to give them up each weekend to your ex-spouse, but be thankful that they are alive.

Consider taking your children with you sometime, depending upon their ages.

"Help others, help yourself" exercise.

Regardless of how desperate your situation appears, look around you and find others who are having a worse time of it than you are. Spend some time every month helping others. When your children are visiting your ex-spouse and you are feeling sorry for yourself, offer to serve meals at your local shelter for the homeless. Take some of your children's outgrown clothes and toys with you to share with others. Inquire about local organizations that help the families of prisoners. In some areas it is called "Project Angel." Adopt a family you can help. Their circumstances are probably much worse than yours. These children are also separated from a parent for reasons they may not understand.

"Be good to yourself" exercise.

Make a list of all the things you like to do and your ex-spouse did not like to do or resented your doing without him or her. Make a list of the activities or interests you gave up when you married your spouse. Make a list of all the things you did because your spouse wanted you to, but which you neither wanted to do or enjoyed doing. Make a list of all the things about you that your ex-spouse disliked. Make a list of all the things about your ex-spouse you disliked.

Start working on each list. Begin doing some of the things you gave up during your marriage, and stop doing the things you didn't want to do. Relish in doing the things that drove your ex-spouse crazy, such as cooking liver or leaving used tissues all over the house. Rejoice that you no longer have to live with all the things you disliked about your ex-spouse.

Library exercise.

Take your children to the library for a family outing. Check out books written especially for their age on divorce and family relationships, and check out some books for yourself on the same topic. Spend time scanning the books for ideas and help even if you think you don't have time to read the entire book. Look at the table of contents and just read areas of interest to you.

After you have gone through the divorce books, keep taking the children to the library. Spend a couple of hours there. Show them children's magazines that they would enjoy reading but which you feel you cannot afford to buy. Sit down and read some magazines in your areas of interest too.

Spending a few hours together at the library can be a meaningful step in your family's growth and recovery. It can be a fun family outing that doesn't cost a penny—unless you forget to return your books on time!

Drawing exercise.

If you have an undeveloped interest in art, express yourself by drawing or painting your concept of divorce. Encourage your children to do the same. Once you have created your artistic rendition of divorce, date it. Each time you have a new concept you want to express, set aside the time to do it, and date it. You will be surprised at the progression of emotions revealed in your paintings and your children's drawings. Even though you think you may be too busy for such frivolous activities, it can be a fun thing for you to do with your kids and another step down your road to recovery.

Fun exercise.

Take some time out for fun. You may be holding down three jobs, having to clean the house, and needing to do the laundry, but occasionally you must take some time off for fun . . . and so must your children. Playing board games, making up stories, reading books, and learning a new skill together can all constitute fun for children. You also need some recreation away from the children. As much as possible, schedule those activities for when your children are with their other parent or when they are doing something with others. Spend as much time as possible with your children. They need this additional security during the divorce recovery process.

Recovery workshop.

Many inexpensive or free workshops are available for adults and children going through divorce. Find out about programs available through your community college, adult education programs, city parks and recreation department, church or synagogue, your children's schools, and other sources. Whether or not you think you have the time and need the assistance, it will give you a boost and afford an opportunity to meet others who are having the same difficulties. Enroll your children in these programs even if they say they don't need them. Ask your school to develop a program for children of divorce. Assist in the process if necessary.

Professional help.

Depending on emotional need, some people should consider getting professional help at the beginning of the divorce process and as often as necessary until healing takes place. A mentally healthy person knows when he or she needs help and seeks it. A mentally unhealthy person will often deny the need for professional help.

Some of these exercises and techniques are simple . . . and you might even find some of them ridiculous. If so, don't do them. They are, however, ideas that many people have found helpful. Try to find one or more that work for you, or create some of your own. This list is simply meant to provide emotional assistance for people who are so devastated by the divorce that they don't know how to help themselves or people who just need some ideas to help them over the rough spots.

People who carry around garbage are toxic people. And this toxicity is contagious, like a disease. So surround yourself with people who are in the process of letting go of the garbage so that you can more effectively get on with your own life.

Until you dump the garbage of negative thoughts and emotions, you won't have the freedom to love and to be joyous again. And be careful not to get into another relationship before you have let go of the garbage of the previous one.

One last suggestion to carefully consider can be the most beneficial to your children. I urge you to put your hostilities behind you and consider having a divorce ceremony.

Divorce involves loss that is often more painful than death. Sometimes funerals ease the pain for the bereaved because they symbolize the finality of death, allowing them to let go. Some couples use a divorce ceremony to finalize the process and reaffirm their love for their children.

If you and your ex-spouse can contain your anger and pain long enough, have a brief ceremony witnessed by family and close friends during which you pledge to your children that just because you don't love each other any more, that doesn't mean you don't love them.

Ask each grandparent, relative, and close friend to attend and affirm verbally to your children that they still love them even though Mom and Dad aren't going to be married any more. Ask your clergyman or a respected neutral party to conduct the ceremony for you.

Some couples have a message written into their divorce agreement. Allison Quattrocchi, of the Family Mediation Center in Scottsdale, shared with us what was written into one couple's divorce agreement:

This shared parenting agreement cannot take into account all the love that we have for you or all the pain that you have experienced. It can't even spell out all the changes that the future holds or give us all the answers.

What this agreement can do is let you know that family relationships don't end when a marriage does, and that we are your parents forever and ever, as long as you want and need us.

We want to thank you for loving us and not taking sides, for being there when we needed a hug or reassurance. You've been wonderful and we could not have asked for anything more than what you've given.

We want you to feel free to love us both, without conflict or fear. We will do our very best to always provide you with the loving support and stability you want and need.

Parents and families are forever. Count on it.

With love, Mom and Dad.[3]

If you are going through a divorce, look inward and introduce yourself to the stranger within. Start rebuilding. Your journey of self-discovery will be the most remarkable voyage you will ever embark upon. Your basis of self-worth is going to be tested. All aspects of your life will be restructured once the rebuilding process begins. Your belief in yourself and in God, your role at home, in the work place, and in society will also be put to the test.

The death of a relationship will open up two roads . . . the road to self-pity and the road to self-discovery. Which road you take will be determined by your attitude. As the initial shock dissipates, the emotional exhaust fumes clear, and the dust on the road settles, you will make the right choice.

The decision is simple; it's time for the negative influences to end. Time to turn the world of negatives into a world filled with new experiences and unlimited promise. There is no other choice. Seize the opportunity to begin a season of new growth.

5

Visitation

I feel like I'm being torn apart. I'm in the middle of a tug-of-war between Mom and Dad. Sometimes I wish I was two people so I could be with both of them, then it wouldn't hurt so bad.
Nine-year-old boy

There is a story in the Old Testament about two women, roommates, both of whom have newborn babies. One night they go to sleep, each with her child cuddled up next to her. During the night, one of the women accidentally rolls over onto her infant, killing it. In her anguish, she resorts to a vile trick—she exchanges her dead child for her roommate's living one, hoping she won't notice.

Of course, when morning comes the second woman realizes the deception and goes straight to King Solomon for help. The two women, standing before the king, each tell a different tale—each one claiming the living child is hers and the dead one the other's.

Solomon, who knows neither woman, uses some trickery of his own. Asking for his sword, he tells the women quite simply that the only way to resolve the dispute is to cut the child in two and give half to one and half to the other. But the woman whose child is still alive blurts out, "O My lord, give her the living child, and by no means kill him!"

The other, however, says, "Let him be neither mine nor yours, but divide him." And of course Solomon instantly realizes that the woman who demonstrated enough compassion to place the interests of the child above all else—even if it meant giving him up—is the genuine parent.

Recast one of these women in the role of the father and the story bears a striking resemblance to a modern-day custody battle. Unfortunately, compassion such as that demonstrated by the mother in this tale is a rare commodity among battling parents, and there is no all-wise king to ensure that the interests of the child are kept paramount. Children become another possession to be divided by the splitting couple, and the kids often feel as if Solomon's sword has whacked them in two, cleaving their loyalties and their hearts.

As bitter and hateful as a protracted custody battle can be, it often pales by comparison to what happens once the courts have handed down their decision. Although the divorce decree has stated explicit conditions for visitation, the enforcement of these guidelines is virtually impossible. Parents tend to interpret a court's ruling in the broadest possible sense, often bending the rules so much as to make them unrecognizable. Mom and Dad are often like a pair of vicious, rival street gangs looking for any opportunity to fight, and the issue of visitation is enough to start a no-holds-barred free-for-all. It is the casting down of the gauntlet.

In this arena the children are used as weapons even though they are, in fact, the victims. And the battle is neither short nor cheap.

A frequent power play by the custodial parent is to make the non-custodial parent beg for the right to use the visitation privileges provided for in the divorce decree. As a general rule, the specifics are laid out, but that doesn't mean both partners will abide by them. As a matter of fact, the custodial parent will often ignore them just to harass the other parent. Regardless of what the decree says, the custodial parent knows that the other parent will have to return to court at great expense to get a court order to see the child. Unfortunately, by the time this all occurs, the important occasion for which the parent wanted the child has already passed. It may have been a family reunion or vacation that was planned, a special holiday or just regular visitation.

Marla chose to use her children as pawns to retaliate against her husband for leaving her for another woman. By court decree, the children were allowed to spend one month with their father during the summer, but she would be allowed to see them for one weekend during that month. The first summer the father exercised his visitation rights, he planned a trip with his kids and his new wife for the second half of the month. During the first half he worked every day and the children were in the care of their stepmother. Every night when he came home, he talked to the children about their upcoming trip and showed them maps and pictures of where they would be going. Anticipation was at its peak when they had to return to their mother's home for the weekend.

Marla, however, refused to return the children when her weekend visit was over. She told the children that their father called and canceled the trip and that they would have to go to a day-care center for the next two weeks while she worked. No matter how hard the father begged her, she would not return the children. She knew that if he went to the expense of going back to his attorney and getting a court order to force her to return the children, he would not have enough money for their vacation. Also, by the time the legal process was complete, his vacation would be over.

For several years Marla continued to circumvent the father's legal visitation rights and seemed to take great delight in only allowing the children to visit when it interfered with special events her ex-husband and his new wife had planned. Unfortunately, the father finally decided it wasn't worth the grief and quit asking to exercise his visitation rights. After five vacation trips were ruined by Marla, he learned not to get his hopes up. He and his wife have learned to enjoy going on vacations by themselves, so the children are the real losers.

Parents who manipulate their children's emotions and allow them to incorrectly believe that the other parent betrayed them, broke promises, or stopped caring about them are woefully lacking in integrity and are not concerned about the best interests of their children.

Some parents, however, believe they have evidence that it is in the best interests of the children to keep them away from the other parent. Instances of child abuse, neglect, or molestation are good reasons to keep your children away from a victimizing parent.

If you haven't already experienced the multiplicity of frustrations and torments that a heated visitation dispute can engender, brace yourself for the blows. Forewarned is forearmed. After reviewing a selection of commonplace errors many parents commit during visitation, we will offer some general guidelines to make visitation a little easier.

6

I wish someone would
tell my dad not to be so
fake when we visit.
                Twelve-year-old girl

Common
Visitation
Mistakes

Visitation can be an awkward, painful experience that is
as hard for the non-custodial parent as it is for the child.
Sometimes it is so emotionally draining that a parent finds
it easier to gradually withdraw from the children rather
than experience the reopening of wounds every time they
visit. Often the children arrive at a parent's home laden
with animosity and bile pummeled into them by a spite-
ful custodial parent, and it may take hours or days to
reestablish some kind of civil relationship with them—
usually just about the time they are supposed to go back
home.

The uniqueness of the visiting relationship is made
clear in *Surviving the Breakup*, a heavily-researched book
by Judith S. Wallerstein and Joan Berlin Kelly. "With
the marital separation, father [or mother] and child both
face an abrupt discontinuity in the form of their daily
contact. Suddenly, they must adapt their mutual feelings
and needs to the narrow confines of the visit."[1]

Mothers seem to endure special problems of their own
when deprived of their children. In the newsletter *Marriage and Divorce Today*, psychologist Janice Katz says,
"For many, the loss of their children leaves them with a
feeling of loss of self. They express a great fear that

because they are no longer seeing their children on a daily basis, they will no longer be considered 'the mother.' "[2] She says that the simple act of shopping for one rather than for the family can be devastating.

The visit—an unnatural event at best—is burdened with trepidation and anxiety. Parents and children who were used to continual exposure to one another are suddenly forced to compress all their feelings into a relatively short time span. Let's look at a few of the common mistakes parents make.

Cramming a flurry of "fun" activities into the visit with little or no time for discussion or closeness. When asked what might make his visits with his father more productive, one teenager simply answered, "Communication."

Consider the example of a non-custodial father named Jack. Devastated by his divorce and loaded with guilt, he determined to make his kids' visit a nonstop whirlwind of activity. From Saturday morning to Sunday night, his kids roller-skated, went to the movies, played basketball, ate at nice restaurants, and generally whooped it up. Although his kids reported what a great time they were having—they even saw more of him now than before the divorce—they were not exposed to each other in a realistic way. The artificial environment in which they lived each weekend prohibited real interaction, and each missed out on the growth and development of the other.

Such behavior by the non-custodial parent leads children to the false conclusion that if they were to live with a father like Jack, life would be just like the weekend every day of the week. The parent providing all the thrills becomes the "good guy," and the other parent—the one who dispenses discipline—becomes the "meanie."

No enforced responsibilities or discipline. This point is a natural consequence of the first, but even if children are not provided with nonstop entertainment, it can still occur.

Joe just couldn't seem to overcome his guilt about

leaving his ex-wife for his new love. When his ten-year-old and fifteen-year-old daughters visited, he refused to make them do anything they didn't want to do. Even though they were with him all summer long, he never laid any ground rules or reprimanded either of them. Their beds were left unmade, they snacked and left food and dirty dishes all over the house, and they let their clothes and other possessions accumulate on the furniture. When Joe's wife asked the children to pick up after themselves, they threatened, "If we have to help, we're not ever coming here again." Joe insisted she not pester them anymore. When they realized their ploy had worked, the children carried their liberties to extremes. They watched television all day and never showered or dressed until Joe came home and invited everyone out to dinner. Again, this is an artificial atmosphere and can make the custodial parent appear wicked and tyrannical when he or she is forced to reinstate a code of conduct that was cast aside during the visit . . . to say nothing about how unfair it is to the stepmother.

This action not only engenders negative feelings toward the custodial parent, but it also plants seeds of rebellion in the children. When Mom tries to make them clean their room, they now have a weapon to use against her, "Well, Dad doesn't make us do that." Whereas before they probably would have obeyed, albeit not without complaints, now they have a reason to issue an outright challenge to the authority of the custodial parent.

Doing what the visiting parent wants without consideration for what the children enjoy or want. Without meaning to be inconsiderate, many parents assume that their kids will enjoy the same things they do. If a father's favorite Sunday activity is a football game on TV, he may inadvertently force a child whose greatest love is ballet into three grueling hours of boredom.

Diane began to complain every time a visit with her father drew near. When her mother asked why, she said, "Because I get tired of having to fix food and drinks and take it to Daddy and my brother while they watch sports on TV all the time.''

Dr. Richard A. Gardner, in his book *The Parents' Book About Divorce*, explains these parents as follows:

> They may drag the children along on business visits, seat them at an office desk for hours on end to amuse themselves as best they can, or prop them up in front of the television set for as long as they will tolerate it. The children may resent being so neglected but may be fearful of expressing their anger, lest they see even less of the parent.[3]

Remember that your visit is a special, limited time and should not be frittered away on activities you could do another day.

Doing what the kids want without consideration for what the parent wants and enjoys. This is the flip side of the last problem.

John catered to the children's every whim during each visitation period. When one activity ended he always asked them what they wanted to do next, then did it. It wasn't long before his patience was overtaxed. After a few too many games of goofy golf and an overdose of horror movies, he began to resent spending his entire weekend doing things he didn't want to do. Even though he never complained to the kids, his resentment surfaced as grouchiness, yelling, and flying off the handle over tiny violations of his perception of good behavior. The children didn't understand why he never seemed to be in a good mood.

The quality of the time John spent with his children was undermined, and soon he drifted away from them by scheduling business appointments on the weekend and finding excuses to leave the house on one errand or another. Eventually, the visits were less frequent and shorter. How could he justify two mind-numbing days of childish activity?

The imbalance of fun activities, discipline, and real parent-child interaction once again manifests itself as a visit in an unrealistic setting, creating a lack of communication on both sides.

Everybody does his or her own thing. The story repeats itself here with a twist. When either the parent or the children have their way, someone suffers. But when everyone goes off in different directions, the visit between non-custodial parent and child makes no sense whatsoever. It is reduced to a mere ritualistic act by both parties. One can envision both parent and child, if asked how the visit was, to simply mumble, "Fine."

When Ralph picks up his kids, they usually bring along some toys and, more often than not, a friend or two. During the entire visit, Ralph and his new wife go about their normal household routine and pursue their own interests as if the kids weren't there. Because the children are accustomed to it, they ignore their father, watch a lot of television, and spend the night at friends' homes. Nobody shares anything with anyone, and the visit is a waste.

One teen said that simply "doing more things together" would make the difference between a good visit and a bad one.

Infrequent, inconsistent visiting habits. Even though decreed by the courts, as mentioned in the introduction, visitation can break down in reality. Getting off to a bad start sometimes ruins the parent-child relationship permanently. According to Wallerstein and Kelly:

> The relationship between visiting father and child is at its most malleable immediately after the father has moved out of the household and as the visiting pattern emerges. The foundations of the new visiting relationship are laid down during the immediate post-separation period. If weakened at this time, the relationship may be more difficult to restore. But visiting parent and child also have a second chance at this

critical juncture, a chance to break free of past unhappy relations and establish a new bond between father and child.[4]

How often a child comes into contact with his or her
parents following a divorce is a key factor in the time
required to recover from all the trauma. Several studies
reveal that the percentage of children living with their
natural mothers who *never* see their fathers is as high as
46 percent. One child who was asked how often he sees
his father replied, "He comes once every three years to
make himself known again."

The confusion for kids who don't see their non-
custodial parent regularly is evidenced in the following
quotes:

"I don't know where he is or even if he is alive."

"When my dad left I never saw him again." This from
a fourteen-year-old girl whose parents divorced ten years
earlier.

"I only see him once or twice a year because of his
job."

When asked what might make this relationship better,
the children's answers resembled one another:

"To see him more often."

"Longer visits."

"To spend more time with him."

Obviously, there are a multitude of reasons why a parent might not visit regularly—hostile ex-spouses, distance, and scheduling problems to name a few. But as
far as the responsibility lies with you as non-custodial
parent, every attempt should be made to let your children
know you care for them and are interested in them.

As far as scheduling conflicts go, Gardner writes:

Parents do well to appreciate that stipulated visitation
times do not generally coincide with the needs and
desires of the parties concerned. Accordingly, the more
flexible the schedule, the more natural the visits will

be, and the greater the likelihood the visitation experiences will be gratifying. Such flexibility requires a certain amount of trust and cooperation between the parents. Sadly, these conditions are often not present, and the greater the degree of distrust and antagonism, the lengthier and more detailed the schedules become.[5]

Gardner goes on to suggest that a way to avoid scheduling crises is to make visits shorter and more frequent, rather than spend hours feuding with an ex-spouse over how to fit a lengthy stay into everyone's schedule.

7

Guidelines for Visitation

I always feel like there's something missing when I visit Dad. Sometimes I feel like a prisoner. . . . He's so hard to understand.
Fourteen-year-old girl

We have already commented that visitation is, by its very nature, an unnatural phenomenon. With all the trappings of the "typical" family cast aside, the visiting parent and child enter a twilight zone where everyone is trying to act as if nothing has happened, but everyone is painfully aware that something has. Some people refer to this as the "Zoo Father" or "Disneyland Dad" syndrome.

Wallerstein and Kelly state:

> The part-time parent and the part-time child often begin with a bewildering sense of no place to go and no idea of what to do together. The relationship is from the outset beset by practical problems: by the presence of children of different ages and colliding interests; by the absence of the mother who had often served as an interpreter of the children's needs. To many fathers these practical problems seemed at first insurmountable.[1]

And, indeed, the same is true of non-custodial mothers. Where prior to divorce a parent and child may have shared a perfectly natural, easy relationship, during a visit they may resort to a lot of staring at the ground and shuffling of feet. The constraints of time and worries about what they will do together—problems they never had before—are suddenly all they can think of.

In this section we will consider a few general tips to remove many of the obstacles a visiting parent and child face, then consider pickups and deliveries, holiday visitation, the needs of grandparents, and visiting for the absentee parent.

General Principles

Allow life to go on as usual. Don't pretend you don't have responsibilities or commitments that must be handled. Include your children in as many of them as possible. If you are mowing the lawn, let the kids help you empty the grass catcher, sweep the sidewalk, and haul off the grass. If you need to make minor household repairs, walk through each step with them so it is a learning experience for them. The general idea here is to show the child that you have adapted to a new lifestyle and your repertoire is as familiar and routine to you as was your lifestyle in your previous marriage. Encourage your child to become a part of that lifestyle and to feel at ease with it.

Set aside some time to be alone with each child. You don't need to go any place special, but give each child an opportunity to talk to you without any interruptions from others, even if it just involves a short period of time such as reading a story and tucking them in bed without anyone else present. Ask them what is happening in their lives, and share your feelings with them. Give each child your undivided attention for that time.

When you see your children on a regular basis, such as every other weekend, occasionally allow them to bring a friend over to spend the night or arrange to have a friend over for the afternoon to play. It will relieve part of the unnaturalness of the situation and allow the child to play in your home environment just like he or she would at home with the custodial parent. This is espe-

cially important if a third party is being introduced to
the child. If the dad wants the children to meet his significant other, it is a good idea to say, "Next weekend I
am going to have a friend go with us to the zoo or on a
picnic, so would each of you like to invite one of your
friends also?" This can remove some of the resentment
and make the transition to the new relationship a bit
smoother.

Frequently children are frightened after a divorce and
desperately need quality time with the absent parent. The
most critical part of the visitation time occurs between
you and your child and need not involve anyone else.
This often means leaving your significant other or new
marriage partner out of the picture. If a child feels replaced by your new love interest, he or she will resent
the person and will make present and future relationships
very difficult. Gradually bring the new stepparent into the
picture, but always be sure to leave time for just you and
your son or daughter. Employing this technique will prevent many problems.

Discipline your children with love. If they are misbehaving or need to be corrected, don't feel like they will
get mad at you and want to go home if you discipline
them. Children will respect you more if you make them
mind. (Refer to the chapter on discipline in this book.)
A realistic, natural-as-possible life during visitation cannot be achieved if the rules by which a child lives are
lifted for no other reason than to relieve a parent's guilty
feelings about the divorce.

*Assign responsibilities to your children while they are
visiting, and make sure they do them.* Again, we are
striving for reality here. Regardless of how they complain at the time, they will appreciate it later.

Jeannie came from a very wealthy family. Both her
mother and father had full-time maids after the divorce.
Jeannie lived with her mother, but her mother never made
her do any chores. She didn't even have to make her bed.
However, when Jeannie spent the summer with her father

and his new wife, her "mean old stepmother" told the maid not to clean Jeannie's room and bathroom. She showed Jeannie how to do it and made sure it was clean every day. Jeannie also had to help with the cooking, do the dinner dishes, and clean up the kitchen. And she complained daily about it.

However, Jeannie now has her own home and it is spotless. Her mother, on the other hand, doesn't have a maid anymore and her home is a mess. She never learned how to clean house or make it look nice. Jeannie is very thankful to her stepmother for making her accept the responsibility of taking care of her own room and teaching her how to clean and cook.

Ask your children what special things they would like to do while visiting you. Encourage them to make a list. During each visit, select one special event or activity you can do away from the house and one event you can do at home together.

If the children don't come up with their own list, suggest some things you think would be fun to do together. For example:

• Select a book or series of books, and read part of it out loud to your children each time they visit. Don't allow them to take the book home and read ahead of you— reserve it for your special times together. Depending upon their ages, some good books to consider are: *The Incredible Journey, The Hardy Boys* mystery series, *Nancy Drew* mysteries, *Miss Minerva and William Green Hill*, or any other favorites, including adventure stories, classic children's literature, and picture books.

• Learn a new skill together. Some skills can be learned through trial and error and others may require group lessons through your local YMCA, civic activity centers, or other local groups. For a few laughs, allow your child to teach you a new skill such as roller-skating, ice-skating, or tennis. It will be great fun for all and a wonderful way to spend good quality time together.

When Mike was ten his father was awarded custody, and Mike only saw his mother during school vacations since they lived several thousand miles apart. Mike's mother was able to spend more on him than his father could, so each Easter vacation she would do something special with Mike. Sometimes she would choose the activity and other times he would. Much to Mike's surprise, his mom arranged for them to learn how to snow ski. Neither one had ever skied before, but they took lessons and spent a wonderful week together in the snow. As Mike grew older it became his favorite sport. Whenever possible, he would ski with his mom, but whether she was there or not, he always had wonderful memories of the hilarious time they had together watching each other slide and tumble down the ski slopes.

• Work on a project together, either something that can be completed during one visit or carried on for several years.

Sean's father bought a car for him when he was ten years old. However, the car didn't run and it needed to be totally renovated. Since his dad loved to work on old cars, he thought it would be a fun, educational experience for Sean to help him restore the car. Sean was delighted. Each weekend they would take one part of the car and spend time repairing, cleaning, looking for parts, or otherwise consuming themselves with the car. For five years they stretched out the renovation project. By the time Sean was old enough to get his driver's permit, he knew more about the internal workings of his car than most people who had driven for years. When he was sixteen, his father gave him the car—a wonderful reminder of many long hours together sharing their lives.

• If restoring a car isn't your particular cup of tea, virtually any activity two people can do together will suffice. Take a walk or a bike ride together. The simple things in life afford the most opportunity for sharing. Get to know your children while you are walking. Ask about their hopes, their dreams, their school friends, their teachers, and what they are learning in school. Find out which TV programs they watch, what books they read, and what kind of music they like.

• What do fathers do with their daughters? It's really not too hard: Find out what kinds of things they are interested in and do what you can to develop an interest in them too. Suzanne became interested in crossword puzzles, jigsaw puzzles, and paper sculpture. Her father arranged to find unique ones they could enjoy working on together and, in the process, acquired a new hobby.

Sarah and her dad worked on a memory book together. They took pictures of many of the things they did together and compiled them into a scrapbook.

Natalie and her father made up songs when they were together. She loved to sing the themes from various TV programs and change the words to fit their family members. A good place to start is with the theme from "The Brady Bunch," which kids of all ages still watch in reruns. See how creative you and your kids can be with this theme song or any other song or commercial jingle they like.

Wendy loved to collect many different items ranging from shells to miniatures. Each time she visited her dad they spent some time looking around for something unique to add to one of her collections. She had a story to tell about each item—where they found it and how long they looked.

Halie shares her father's interest in music. Each time they get together they enjoy browsing through music stores learning about new releases and expanding each other's knowledge of the type of music they like. At home they listen to different artists' renditions of the same songs and make tapes and fake "commercials" using their music library.

Although it's hackneyed, it's really true that quality of time counts more than quantity. Listen to your children more than you talk to them. Don't dwell on how little or how much time you have together—as far as you are able, try to eliminate all concepts of time, making the visit less pressured. Fully experience and savor every moment you have together, listening, observing, and reserving judgments. Get to know everything about your children.

Avoid the temptation of asking your children to tell you what is going on in your ex-spouse's personal life. Don't ask the children any questions that might make them feel like they are betraying the other parent if they answer. Refer to the chapter on how divorce affects children.

Be careful about how you talk about your ex-spouse to your children. When Joe would talk to his son Forrest about the divorce, he always framed Forrest's mother, Linda, as the villain and *never* referred to her as Forrest's mother. It was always, "Linda left us on our own," "Linda ran off with another man," or "Linda just doesn't care about us anymore." Throughout his early teens, Forrest was constantly hearing how "bad" Linda was. Often when his mother would call, Forrest would not want to talk with her; and when he would visit her, truly constructive communication was impossible until Forrest had spewed forth the negative images and thoughts about his mother—usually in a tearful argument. And then, after the argument, neither Forrest nor his mother felt like sharing anything constructive.

Yet when Forrest reached his later teens and began to think and discern more maturely, he realized that while his father, Joe, had been right about his mother leaving, that was not the reason for his parents' divorce. The real reason was that his parents did not understand nor love each other—and, in that sense, both of them were equally "guilty" for the divorce. But in understanding this, Forrest also realized that his father's incessant negative comments about his mother had, in essence, prevented him from having a close relationship with his mom. Thus while Joe may have captured his son's loyalties on a temporary basis, it cost him the respect of his son as a thinking adult.

Never ask the children to convey messages for you,

especially ones that will upset the custodial parent. There is no need to shoot a barb into your ex-spouse with a message such as, "The child support check is going to be late this month." Matters pertaining to the divorce and the children should be handled by the spouses over the telephone without getting the children involved. Remember not to use your child as a weapon. Also, never send money to the ex-spouse by your children.

Although Jennifer is thirty years old now, her most vivid memory of her parents' divorce is what transpired when she returned from her very first visit with her father twenty-two years ago. Jennifer's dad planned a very special weekend filled with lots of surprises. It included an introduction to her brand-new twenty-one-year-old stepmother and a trip for three to a ski lodge in his brand-new Porsche. Jennifer added a couple of surprises of her own to the package. During the weekend she broke both legs skiing.

When Dad returned an almost paralyzed Jennifer home to her mother, Jennifer got to break the news, "Mom, Dad and his new wife took me skiing, in his new Porsche, and I broke both of my legs." To this day, all Jennifer remembers afterward was seeing her mother sob for several hours. She felt that somehow it must have been her fault.

Eliminate the temptation to be offended if your children don't want to come see you sometimes when they have special plans with their friends. Stan should win a "Good Father" award in this category. Each week he checks with his kids to see if they have any school parties or activities they want to attend or if they want to invite a friend over to spend the weekend with them. He works his schedule around driving them to and from the party or event and never gets offended if it infringes on his visitation time.

Peer relations are extremely important to children. Part of their healing process is to get on with their life, and you must do the same. If they have other plans, find something to do that makes you feel good about yourself, and realize how you'd feel if you were them.

Do something special with each child without the others around. Occasionally arrange to pick up only one of your children, and spend a few hours doing something special with that child which the other children might not enjoy. This can make your visits more pleasant and provide an opportunity to find out how the child is feeling. If you treat your kids as one collective entity, you negate their individuality. Ask your kids if there is anything special they would like to do with you by themselves or offer a few suggestions.

Diane always wanted to go to work with her father. Each summer he would arrange to take her with him for one day on his bakery delivery route. Diane loved to ride in the truck with him and help him carry in the products to the store. Her dad introduced her to all his customers and everyone was especially nice to her and often gave her small treats from their stores. Her brothers and sisters had no interest in going, so it was a special treat reserved for Diane.

Diane's brother, Todd, wanted to spend a day fishing with his dad without all his sisters around. So once each summer, Todd and his dad would get up early and spend the entire day fishing, without Todd worrying about sharing his dad's attention with his sisters.

Sarah, Diane's older sister, loved to go out to eat all by herself with her father. They would go to a fancy restaurant and have a good time talking and sharing about what was happening in each other's lives. Sometimes they would go to a concert afterward, or to a movie or shopping, but it was Sarah's special time with her father.

Children are fearful of losing their parents' love and don't want to compete with their siblings. As often as possible arrange to do something special with just one child, but be sure to do the same—in quality and quantity—with each. Family time can be a time of insecurity when one or more of the children feel uncertain about their place in the family or loss of one parent's love.

8

I wish we could all live in the same town instead of so far away. We hardly ever get to see Dad because it costs too much.

Eight-year-old boy

When a Child Has to Travel

Both custodial and non-custodial parents often deliberately antagonize their ex-spouse by making visitation as difficult as possible. When both parents are in the same vicinity the results are not as devastating as when it involves expensive travel or a considerable amount of travel time to pick up the children.

Robert lived with his father, five hundred miles from his mother, Jane. She was going to school and only had part-time employment. Jane was not eligible for vacation time but arranged to visit Robert over a long weekend. His father would not allow him to leave the state to go see his mother, but allowed her to visit Robert in the town where he lived. The date and time were arranged and confirmed the day before she left. Jane drove ten hours to pick up her son so she could see him for two days before she drove ten hours back home.

However, when Jane arrived at the house to pick up Robert, she was informed by his dad that he had decided at the last minute to let him go visit his grandparents in another city four hundred miles in the opposite direction.

When Jane finally reached Robert on the phone, he told her his dad said she had decided not to come see him so he could go visit his grandparents.

70

Because similar situations had happened so frequently in the past, Jane was unable to get angry. She was so numb she couldn't even feel anger. Intensely disappointed at not being able to see her son after a rough week of school and work, plus a ten-hour drive, Jane got a motel room, slept for twenty hours, got in the car and spent another ten hours driving back home.

She went back to court for another expensive attempt to make Robert's father abide by the visitation guidelines. But before the hearing, Robert's dad moved him once again to another state two thousand miles from her. Robert's father agreed to allow him to fly to see his mother whenever she could afford it.

Flying makes it easier on the parents, but it can be very tough on the kids. We want to share with you a letter written by a flight attendant that was printed in Ann Landers's column on November 2, 1987. It is entitled "Solo Flights Often Turbulent for Children."

Dear Ann Landers: I am a flight attendant for a major airline and can no longer put off writing this letter.

We flight attendants see so many children from broken families and have concluded that too many parents are looking for the easy way out.

The little ones look brave when Mom or Dad sends them off and when they're met at the other end, but don't think for a minute that the flight is easy for them. They are still children. I can see the frightened eyes of a dozen or more youngsters that I have cuddled and reassured on cross-country flights.

Parents take for granted that the person sitting next to their child will assume parental duties, or that a flight attendant will be assigned to care for their youngster. It doesn't always work that way.

On yesterday's flight, I had to move a little girl because some passengers overheard the man next to her using obscene language. Last week, I had to move another little girl because the man next to her was holding her in a way that made my skin crawl. He said she was cold.

Two weeks ago I sent eleven children off with one arrival agent through a crowded New York airport. Anyone who thinks one agent can take eleven children safely through a crowded airport doesn't know anything about children.

Please tell your readers that if they plan to send a child alone on a plane because it's more convenient, please reconsider. If a parent must send a child alone for financial reasons, we will do our best to take care of that youngster, but parents should be aware of the dangers. If I had a child, I wouldn't do it.—Life at thirty-thousand feet.

Ann Landers responded:

Dear Life: As a frequent flier, I have seen many of the children you have written about. However, the other side of the story looks like this: Many divorced parents can't afford to accompany their children and fly back alone. Sending them solo is better than depriving them of the visit.

Thanks for calling attention to a problem that needs to be aired. Flight attendants around the world will bless you.[1]

When children under twelve travel with an adult, they pay less than full fare. Children who fly alone pay full fare because the airlines have a greater responsibility for them. Another thing to be aware of is that human error is as prevalent as computer error. We have heard and seen many stories about how children were overlooked, put on the wrong plane, or left stranded by themselves in a major airport.

A friend of ours has sent her daughter, Sandy, on long-distance flights to see her father four times a year for ten years. On approximately 25 percent of the flights there was a major slip-up by the airlines, and the child was left alone and bewildered, not knowing what to do.

Another friend has sent her son, Chad, by himself on more than fifty flights to visit his father. His record is about the same. On eight different occasions the airlines slipped up and lost track of him when they changed crews and planes at the Los Angeles airport. Fortunately, his parents had taught him what to do when left alone while changing planes.

If money is not a factor, have a neutral adult fly with the child to and from the destination. In some families a friendly aunt or uncle goes along so the child does not experience separation anxiety or fear of abandonment.

But if your children have to travel on a plane by themselves, follow these guidelines:

1. Write their name, address, and phone number on a stick-on label and stick it inside their jacket or sweater.
2. Make sure they know how to call you or another relative long distance and have two dollars worth of change to use the pay phone in case they are lost in the shuffle.
3. Show them how to identify the uniforms of the personnel of the airline they are traveling on. Tell them to go to one of these people and tell them they need help.
4. Help them identify airport security personnel, and show them how to locate them.
5. Show them where the paging phones are, and tell them how to use them and locate them in other airports.
6. Always allow them to travel with one of their favorite toys or books.

Parents should also realize that no matter how strong the temptation, they should never use the last two minutes before boarding as the close personal time with their child that they might not have shared during the visit. The child is about to be placed all alone into a hostile environment (hostile in the sense that everyone and everything on the plane is not a part of the child's normal world), and the last thing the child needs to see before boarding is a parent sobbing. The parent is the child's lifeline on that plane, and if the lifeline is cut or frayed, the trip will be that much more painful. Certainly it is important to let your child know how hard it is for you to put him or her on the plane. However, share your feelings with your child several hours before the trip. Talk out your feelings and share your love while at home before leaving for the airport.

Once at the airport, your objective should be to make the trip as comfortable as possible for your child. Arrange with the flight attendants to pre-board with your child. Get to know the flight crew together, look into the cockpit and tell the pilot "Hello," and then find your child's seat with him or her. Before you leave the plane, show your child where you will be standing inside so that he can wave to you as the plane backs out of the gate.

Just the fact that your child knows you are waiting inside in case the plane doesn't leave right away is important. At all costs, minimize the time your child spends alone—and a child who can wave to a parent through a window is not alone. Similarly, make sure that you are *on time* to pick up your children. There is nothing worse for a child than to stand by watching other families and friends greet one another and see no sign of his or her parent. Often the child will feel compelled to make excuses to the flight attendant about the tardy parent for fear that the flight attendant will assume that the parent just doesn't care. This is not only inconsiderate, it is unhealthy for the child.

Finally, when your children fly alone, always try and

leave them with a happy thought about their visit that they can dwell on during the first part of the flight. Flying alone is a traumatic process for young children—do everything within your power to make their flight easier.

9

Holidays

Holidays are the saddest time of the year for me. If I'm with Mom, I miss Dad and know Dad is sad. If I'm with Dad, I miss Mom and know Mom is home crying. What's a guy supposed to do?

Eight-year-old boy

Holidays are often the roughest periods following a divorce. Children feel intense pain over not being able to spend them with both parents. The parent who does not have the children during the holidays may experience loneliness and depression. Just thinking of happier days when they were all a family makes the present holiday even more painful. The Ghost of Holidays Past—in the form of depression, guilt, and remorse—haunts everyone.

Many divorce decrees stipulate that the children spend alternate holidays with each parent. Every other Christmas and Thanksgiving is spent with Mom. If the parents live close together and are somewhat civil to each other, some experts suggest holding two Thanksgiving dinners and two Christmas dinners, one early and one late in the day, and allow the children to attend each. Above all, avoid the issue of who belongs to whom, and if gift exchanging is part of the holiday, don't get into jealous fights over the value of presents. Some parents try to outdo each other in the amount they spend on the children, but most frequently one parent has considerably more financial ability than the other. Wise parents will coordinate what they are buying to make sure the child isn't giving each parent the same "wish list" and to ensure the needed items are received. If duplicate gifts are received, then the child has the dilemma of whose feelings to hurt by exchanging one of the presents. Careful planning, once again, is the key.

For those who live many miles apart, however, every other Christmas may mean they don't see the child from September until spring vacation if it isn't their year to have the child. Both parent and child experience lots of sadness during the first few holidays they do not get to see each other, and often the reverse is true—holidays may be the only time a parent sees a child. Said one girl of her father, "It's like we're strangers because he only comes on Christmas and there isn't any trust between me and him."

Try to at least make phone contact with your children on the holidays when you cannot be with them. Arrange to have their extended family call them also—just for a few minutes so it doesn't irritate the parent they are with. If that isn't possible, tape a holiday message and send it to them so that they can at least hear the voices of their other loved ones. Also, send a photograph of the family members left behind, plus one or two of their favorite toys or their treasured blanket or pillow.

A fun alternative to getting depressed over not being with your children for special occasions is to celebrate an "unholiday" when you are with them, regardless of what the calendar says. This is the "Christmas in July" concept.

Natalie lives more than two thousand miles from her father. Since her birthday is in October, she was never able to celebrate with her father. So each summer, her father would set a date to celebrate her birthday. All of his relatives would come over for her "birthday" party. They would bring presents, sing "Happy Birthday," give her a birthday cake, and let her blow out the candles just as if it were the real thing. It was a great thing for both father and daughter. When her real birthday came around, both of them had fond memories of sharing her "birthday." Even though she couldn't be with him on the real day, she knew he was thinking of her and had already done his part.

Some families who only see their children every other Christmas also set aside another calendar day for that. They decorate a tree (artificial, depending on the season) and have all the family gathered to share gifts. Pretending it is Christmas can be even more fun than the real thing. You can make all the foods associated with the holidays, play Christmas music, and carry out all your family holiday traditions. Although it might seem silly to those who have never been separated from their children during the holidays, to others who have gone through the despair of loneliness and longing for their children on those special days, it makes a lot of sense. It makes the pain a little more bearable for parent and child.

If you are privileged enough to be with your children during a holiday, encourage them to call your ex-spouse. This will engender more civil relations between you and your ex-spouse, help relieve the sense of loneliness and guilt that your children may be feeling because they can only be with one parent, and ingratiate you to your children as they grow older and begin to understand the resolve and courage that it required of you.

To promote the general welfare and foster a more friendly relationship with your ex-spouse, encourage your children to do something special for their other parent's birthday if they are visiting you close to that time. Many parents never give the children an opportunity to do something for the other parent's birthday or even make holiday gifts. Teaching children to be considerate in this manner is very important.

Remind the children a few days in advance of the other parent's birthday and offer your assistance. Ask them if they would like you to help them find a card or if they are planning to make a card or gift. Offer to take the children shopping or buy something in their name. Offer your assistance in mailing or delivering the card or gift.

Even if finances are very tight, try to part with a few dollars so they can buy a token gift for the other parent. If you are unable to do so, let them know in advance that if they can bring a little bit of money from their savings you will take them to the store to buy an inexpensive gift for their other parent. Even a five-dollar gift that the children can give in their name may be the most important gift the parent receives that year. Many non-custodial parents have never received any kind of a birthday or Christmas card or gift from their children even though they have made a special attempt to take the children shopping for a gift or card for the custodial parent.

This area provides an excellent opportunity for stepparents to gain acceptance in a child's life. When Scott was nine, he went to visit his dad for a few weeks and to meet his new stepmother. Armed with lots of hostility toward the woman who caused his dad to leave his mom, he made up his mind not to like her. Shortly after he arrived she took him shopping and said, "Let's buy a nice present for your mom and send it to her as a gift from you. I know she really misses you and is lonesome for you now." Needless to say, lots of negative feelings were neutralized between Scott and his stepmother.

Gift giving is an important part of a child's development. Children should be encouraged to give gifts they have purchased with their own money or that they have made themselves. More likely than not, the best gifts will not cost much. Here are some suggestions for a gift for the other parent.

- Help them make an audio tape of Mom's or Dad's favorite songs. Or make an audio tape of the children reciting the things they like best about the other parent. Include their ages and the date so it will truly be a keepsake for the parent. Keep the tape focused on the happy times.

- Buy some colored paper and pens and let the children design gift coupons to give to the other parent. The coupons can be promises to do certain things without complaining, such as:

  - I promise to keep my room clean for a week.
  - I promise to take a bath without being told.
  - I promise to do the dishes for you when you are especially tired.

Encourage older children to give coupons such as:

  - I promise to wash the car.
  - I promise to clean the garage.
  - I promise to clean and organize the kitchen cupboards.

Some gifts that cost around five dollars include: a key chain, framed school pictures, gourmet food items such as flavored coffee, specialty nuts or candy, flavored popcorn, or caramel apples. Another fun thing for kids to do is bake some of the other parent's favorite cookies.

Whether or not you have forgiven your ex-spouse, you don't want your children to sense any animosity. Although it might be difficult for you to assist the children in gift giving for your ex-spouse, it is a *sign of healing and progressing to the next stage of recovery*.

A final caveat concerning your children and the treatment of holidays is a reminder to avoid using them as pawns. As kids become teenagers and get into college, they have more choice about where they will spend their holidays. Fighting over who gets the kids doesn't stop when they turn eighteen. Unfortunately, many parents tend to bribe them with attractive packages or trips if they choose to visit them rather than the other parent.

Some fathers promise ski trips during the holidays, and mothers promise wonderful shopping trips for new school clothes. It makes it very painful for the kids to choose, especially if the parents live in different towns far apart. Many kids choose not to spend the holidays with either parent rather than hurt one's feelings.

If you are the parent left without your children during the holidays, don't allow yourself to wallow in self-pity. Go out and perform a community service. Help those who are less fortunate than you or who have no one. Visit children's hospitals and see how many children are alone if their families live out-of-state. Visit a nursing home, or help serve Christmas dinner at your local shelter for the homeless. After my divorce, I found this was the only way I could survive Christmas without my children. Each Christmas I visited a nursing home and took a carnation for each resident. I cried along with the patients as they told me how lonely they were and how much they missed their families. Many were dying alone. It made me feel fortunate to be healthy and alive and able to give joy and a hug to the elderly sick people in the nursing home.

You don't have to be alone to make this a worthwhile activity. Involving your children in these activities with you may be one of the greatest contributions you can make to their lives. Help them appreciate what they have, regardless of how underprivileged they may feel.

10	I wish someone would sit my dad down and say "Look at your daughter! She's almost grown and you've missed most of it."
Between Visits	Fourteen-year-old girl

Even when both parents are cooperative and live in the same area, it's not always easy to adhere to a rigid visitation schedule. As children get older they have a variety of school and social activities that interfere with visitation times. Parents also have work and social commitments that don't always coincide with scheduled visits. But when non-custodial parents live hundreds or even thousands of miles away, it's only natural that parents feel helpless and impotent.

When asked why their fathers don't visit them regularly, most children said it was because he was so far away. Some said, "Because he lives one hundred miles away," and others said, "Because it takes two hours to get there by car." One teenager even said there were "no visits. Mom doesn't want him around, and the law says he can't see us."

For a variety of economic, legal, and logistical reasons, it often simply isn't possible for a non-custodial parent to have extensive contact with his or her children. The solutions to this problem—whether your ex-spouse and you get along or not—center around thoughtfulness, a good memory, and persistence.

In his book, *101 Ways to Be a Long-Distance Super-*

Dad, George Newman offers a list of do's and don'ts. He encourages the absent parent to do the following:

- Cooperate with your ex-wife and "establish a program for communicating with as well as visiting your children."
- Arrange phone conversations in advance, either with your ex or directly with the children if they're old enough.
- Avoid spending exorbitant sums trying to "buy" your children. "Remember," says Newman, "part of being a good parent requires giving of yourself—sometimes a lot. A checkbook simply won't do."[1]

The rest of the book makes good reading for parents—fathers and mothers—who can't be near their kids. Other suggestions include keeping in touch by contacting your child's schoolteachers, doctors, and coaches, deluging your child with mail, planning future vacation times, and making liberal use of the telephone.

You can write letters to your children regardless of their age. If they are too young to read, cut out cartoons or pictures of animals or things they love, paste them on a piece of paper, and just make a one-line comment such as, "This cute little kitten reminded me of you and how much I love to cuddle you. Missing you, Love Dad."

Keep a calendar of important events in the life of your child. *Never* forget birthdays, holidays, or prearranged phone visits. What days are spelling tests? Music lessons? Little League? Children, like adults, love to be remembered.

In your letters, ask your children questions rather than simply listing what you've been doing lately. Make sure the questions are designed to make them feel good about themselves and provoke some good response. Develop mutual interests, and even offer "assignments" so they will be thinking about you between letters and calls and have something to report back. Ask specific questions that they can answer when they write back.

How would you complete this sentence?
What I like best about me is . . .
When I grow up I might want to be a . . .
The thing that is most special about me is . . .

When asked to describe what would improve her relationship with her father, one girl said, "If he would just write me letters and say 'hi' and ask questions about my life and what is going on around it."

Be creative in your contacts with your children. Make them fun rather than obligatory. Play checkers or other games by mail or over the phone. Send your children self-addressed, stamped envelopes so they can respond to you. Make a "contract" with your child to write or call once a week. Teach them how to call you if they are very young. Show them how to call collect if the call is long distance.

In your absence, your children need not grow up unaware of you or how much you love them. Some parents even find that such a rigorous schedule of contact can build a relationship as strong as—perhaps even stronger than—that which develops between a parent and child in intact families.

CONCLUSION

If it seems that we've contradicted ourselves by repeating that visitation is an unnatural phenomenon, while at the same time stressing the importance of making such visits as natural as possible, perhaps an illustration might help.

Consider the difference between a master painter and a photographer. The photographer goes to the Grand Canyon, sets up his tripod, and shoots a perfect likeness of nature. The resulting photograph is completely accurate in detail and is a faultless representation of the subject of the portrait.

Sitting next to the photographer is a painter, his easel set up and his palette a riot of color. After much work and love, he has his own representation of the Grand Canyon, much different in appearance—but no different in value—than the photograph.

The difference between a loving, supportive intact family and a loving, supportive pair of divorced parents is like the difference between the photo and the painting. One is the ideal representation of the family, the other an approximation. Neither need be considered of lesser value.

Following the guidelines in this chapter can lead to a lessening of conflict over a visit with a non-custodial parent—or at least better communication between the absent parent and child—and create that comfortable, "natural" environment.

Wallerstein and Kelly state:

> Successful outcome at all ages, which we have equated with good ego functioning, adequate or high self-esteem and no depression, reflected a stable, close relationship with the custodial parent and the noncustodial parent. . . . In these arrangements, the child or adolescent essentially enjoyed the supports of the intact family.[2]

And from Gardner:

> I believe that they [children] do best when raised with a mother and a father who are relatively happy with one another. To the degree that their arrangement provides this, to that degree they are likely to grow up healthy.[3]

If the divorced parents allow their love for their children to be preeminent and set personal animosities aside,

Solomon's sword can be sheathed and the children can continue to grow and develop in the context of the new, visiting relationship.

Communicating with a Hostile Ex-Spouse

Mom fights with Dad and says bad things to him every time he comes to pick me up. It makes me cry. By the time we leave, Mom is crying and Dad is yelling.

Seven-year-old girl

A major blockade to good visitation between the non-custodial parent and the children is that frequently Mom and Dad get in a big argument when the children are picked up. Placing blame is not necessary. Realizing the universality of it for most couples during the early stages of the divorce is much more helpful. Only after emotions have cooled can the children be picked up and delivered by the ex-spouse without creating a scene. Although it places a damper on the parent picking up the children, it causes more problems for the children.

Such arguments can start over anything and need little or no provocation. Often, both parents are still so hostile toward each other that the seemingly simple act of retrieving their children becomes a battle of mind games. If the kids are happy when Dad picks them up, he interprets it to mean that they are anxious to leave their cruel mother and spend some time with him. If they are unhappy when he arrives, he thinks their depression is the result of the unbearable stress of living with his ex-wife or that his ex-wife is bad-mouthing him. Of course, Mom sees her children's discontent as evidence that they simply hate being with their father. Nobody wins.

Children don't want to leave their mother if they see

her crying and screaming after a fight with their dad. Likewise, they may resent their father for leaving when the visit is over and end up taking sides with their mom.

Most couples don't deliberately seek a confrontation, but until they can get themselves under control, it would be far healthier for the children if a third party picked up and returned the children. If this cannot be arranged, it is a good idea for the custodial parent to stay out of sight when the children are picked up or ask a neighbor to come over to see the children off. If grandparents or other relatives live nearby, consider dropping off and picking up the children there in order to neutralize the emotional damage inflicted upon them. If a third party is used, the third party should not attempt to convey threats or "hate" messages from the other spouse.

Darlene had a very bad temper and always found an excuse to rip apart and run down her ex-husband, Harold, when he came to pick up the children. Since this was part of the reason Harold left, he did not want to be subjected to the screaming and yelling every time he came to pick up or return the children. It always made the children cry, and it took him a couple of hours to get them calmed down during the first part of their visit. Harold was going through chemotherapy at the time and the emotional stress and trauma were more than he could bear.

However, Darlene was determined to extract her pound of flesh so he could reap the consequences of leaving her. Rather than subject himself to it, he asked his new wife to go get the kids for him. This only enraged Darlene further, so she refused to hand the children over to the stepmother.

Rather than subject himself to Darlene's temper, Harold started to give up his visits with the children. Finally, when she was able to get on with her own life and remarry, Darlene was able to be somewhat civil to Harold if her new husband was around when he picked up the children.

Some people feel having a hostile relationship with an ex-spouse is better than none. If the parent who was left doesn't let go of the other parent, possibly the only way he or she can continue the relationship is through anger and hostility, and usually the children are the only avenue by which to do so. When the parent lets go of the hostility, more than likely the relationship has been released also.

The anguish and raw emotions resulting from a divorce do not go away quickly—especially when one person was deserted in favor of another. Realize that World War III potentially awaits you every time you pick up or hand over your children for a visit, and exercise restraint. Again, remember the children are not weapons and the divorce is between you and your ex-spouse. Parents eventually heal as they each get on with their own lives, but hostile attacks and words about and between parents leave emotional scars on the children.

"The visit is an event continually available for the replay of anger, jealousy, love, mutual rejection, and longing between the divorcing adults," say Wallerstein and Kelly. With so many rampant emotions surfacing every time the children change hands, this is the weak point at which the severest wounds can be inflicted. Wallerstein and Kelly continue:

> The fighting between parents occasionally reached pathological, even bizarre, intensity. . . . One father sought a court order requiring his former wife to make herself invisible when he came to the door. All in all, one-third of the children were consistently exposed to intense anger at visiting time. The tension generated by the parents burdened the visits and stressed them and the children.[1]

The use of children as weapons is especially shameful here. Clearly, no child could manage to thrive and become emotionally healthy in this kind of environment.

Attempts at sabotaging the visit can begin long before the doorbell rings and can be practiced by either parent. A father, for example, can "forget" he was supposed to pick up the kids at 7:00—not 8:00—and whatever plans Mom had go out the window. And Mom can suddenly suffer memory loss and has sent the kids off to a friend's to spend the night when Dad arrives to pick them up. Either way, the children lose.

One frequently reported ploy is to send the kids off inadequately clothed or fed. Some custodial parents even have the audacity to send a list of "needed" items with the children, including such "essentials" as cameras and video games. For example, on two different occasions Al and his new wife arranged to have his children fly to southern California for a trip to Disneyland. Al called Suzanne, his ex-wife, to be sure she packed everything the kids needed. Al even offered to come and help the kids pack so there wouldn't be any mistakes. Suzanne refused and insisted on even meeting him at the airport with the kids so she could "see them depart." When they arrived at the Disneyland Hotel and told the kids to put on casual clothes, there were none. Al examined their luggage and found there were no swimsuits, tennis shoes, shorts, or casual clothes. The suitcases were full of clothes that would have been suitable for job interviews at IBM. Needless to say, he had to take them shopping and lay out a considerable sum for items the kids already had back home. The irony was that Suzanne earned far more money than Al. She was simply trying to get even with Al for leaving her for another woman.

Many custodial parents intentionally choose to send their children to the non-custodial parents in ragged clothes and worn-out shoes when they actually have much better clothes at home. Children are used as messengers to relay tales of dire financial situations at home—which may or may not be true. Often the non-custodial parents are forced to buy the children clothes in order to have them look decent for the visit. When children are given money for their extra personal or school needs, the money is frequently confiscated by the custodial parents as soon as they arrive home, rather than remaining the personal property of the children.

Many custodial parents even refuse to allow their ex-spouses visitation rights granted by the courts, relying on the fact that their ex-spouse doesn't have the money to get a court order each time the agreed-upon rights are denied. Unfortunately, the children are used as hostages to inflict torment and anguish. In cases like these, more often than not the non-custodial parent also has tremendous problems trying to communicate with the children, especially in the first two years after the divorce. The problem is compounded when the custodial parent was left for someone else. Mail and gifts are often spitefully intercepted and returned unopened, phone calls are curtailed or denied, and the kids lose a parent.

If the custodial parent is somehow interfering with your ability to communicate or visit your child, be creative. Think of any relatives, friends, or contacts you may have who live near your child and who might pass on letters and messages for you. Grandparents are an ideal example and can, as mentioned above, provide neutral turf. Says Gardner:

> Generally, I advise the parent in such a situation to continue, in a reasonable way, to maintain contact with the children. Letters, presents sent by mail, and telephone calls can often serve well here. Sending messages through friends and relatives can also be useful. Knowing that the parent is still out there, thinking of them, and trying to maintain contact with them is very important for the children's healthy psychological development.[2]

If no one is cordial to you, save the letters to give to your children when they are older.

Children have a right to communicate with either parent whenever they need to. If you are the custodial parent, make it easy for your children to communicate with the non-custodial parent. If you are the non-custodial parent, when the children are visiting you, do not try to hinder their communication with the absent custodial parent. Children love and miss both parents. Just because they are with one parent more than the other doesn't mean they won't miss the custodial parent when they are visiting the non-custodial parent.

Melissa spent every summer out of state with her father, but her father would not allow her to call her mother and would not put through calls from her mother. When the visit was over and she was back home with her mother, she spent a lot of time crying and telling her mother about problems she had during the summer with her father, stepmother, and stepbrothers. Over and over, she said, "I wanted to talk to you so many times but Daddy wouldn't let me." Melissa's mom had told her to try to call collect, but knowing she might try to do so, her father kept the phone locked.

So the next summer they devised a plan. Melissa would get acquainted with the next-door neighbors whose little girl she played with occasionally and ask them if sometimes she could come over and call her mom collect. Melissa also was given a phone credit card and taught how to use it in a pay phone if she could ever get away while they were shopping. By the time she was ten, Melissa became quite adept at finding ways to call her mom.

During the summer Melissa turned eleven, her mother received a phone call that consisted of nothing but crying and sobbing. Melissa was unable to say one word other than "Mommy . . . Mommy . . ."

For more than ten minutes her mom begged her to please tell her what was wrong, but all she could get in response was buckets of sobs. The mother imagined every conceivable problem, but finally found out that Melissa was camping in a state park with her father and stepbrothers when she discovered her period had started.

Not knowing what to do, she managed to get to the camp's pay phone and call her mom. She was too embarrassed to tell her father, and she was scared she was going to bleed to death. Right then she needed to talk to her mom and no one else would do.

Children need to have a way to contact an absent parent. If the parent they are with isn't making it possible, teach them ways to enlist the support of neighbors, friends, or other relatives who will be sympathetic to their plight.

Most often, after a few years the hostility lessens and the parents are not so adamant about keeping the children away from each other. Unfortunately, by the time this happens the absent parent has usually stopped trying to communicate with the children, rather than the other parent preventing it.

Many hostile parents also make the mistake of verbally or nonverbally criticizing their ex-spouse in front of the children. In the long run, it usually hurts the parent making the comments more than the parent it was intended to hurt. Initially the children may believe the remarks, but ultimately they will see that the facts are different from the slurs. How long it takes them to realize the truth will depend on their age, intelligence, social maturity, experiences with the absent parent, and what other people say to them about that parent. Even if all the negative remarks are *true*, it is psychologically destructive for a child to hear one parent criticizing the other. Children know they are a part of each parent. If one of their parents is a terrible person, they think that they must be terrible people too. Experts tell us it is damaging to children's self-esteem to hear their parent continually degraded by the other parent or family members.

Until the angry spouse has forgiven the other person, the children will often be used as pawns, rendering them incapable of making decisions and accepting responsibility until they check with the other parent.

A typical example of this can be seen in Heather. Each

time she visited her father he offered to take her shopping and buy some clothes for her. But when she showed these things to her mom, her mom would go into a tirade about how her dad only bought impractical things and why it was a stupid decision. Heather knew what she liked, but she was so afraid of making her mom mad that she grew incapable of making a decision about anything, even something as small as a pair of shoes. Heather always wanted to call her mom from the store and ask if it was all right for her dad to buy her a pair of shoes she liked. This was one way her mom could continue to exert control over her dad. Doing this to an eight-year-old child is one thing, but when an eighteen-year-old is still incapable of making a decision about what shoes she can own or any other insignificant matter without asking her mother, the child has been emotionally victimized.

Neither the non-custodial parent nor outsiders are going to change the custodial parent when he or she is employing these techniques. All one can really do is make the most of each visitation allowed and ask for help from family and friends.

If you are the subject of the criticism, don't retaliate or try to defend yourself unless the child specifically asks you about the incident. Rather, continue to show your love for the child in every way possible.

If any of this sounds familiar, what can you do? Do you buy your kids the clothes they need during your visit with them? Do you bulldoze your ex-spouse's front door to get at your children? The following tips may help with some of the tougher issues and, above all else, help your children.

1. Don't be discouraged by rebuffs from your ex-spouse. Be tough and determined. If you call enough, the children will be in the room sometime and gradually catch on to what is happening. Pity the poor parent when the child finds out that he or she intercepted your calls and letters.

2. Do everything you can to make contact with your

kids on a regular basis, establishing alternate routes of communication if called for. If your calls or letters aren't getting through, locate a loyal friend or relative to help out, or even send your mail to a private post office box if your children are a little older. Ask someone on your side if you can use their home as neutral territory for a visit or if they will arrange to "run into you" while they are out with your children.

3. Maintain or reestablish contact with your ex-spouse's relatives and friends. State in a positive way what you want for your children, without blaming your ex-spouse for doing bad things to you or them. Without being judgmental, let them know that you feel your letters are not getting through to the children and that you can't reach them by phone. These people can become powerful allies, especially when your long-suffering elicits their admiration and sympathy. Use "I" messages. For example, "I miss my children very much and believe they also miss me. I believe it is important to their emotional welfare to be loved by both parents. I would appreciate anything you could do to convince my ex-spouse to allow me to see the children."

Ask them if they would tell you when your children will be visiting their home and allow you to call there to talk to them or let your kids call you from their house. Perhaps you can send your letters to your kids there as well. If the relatives are aware of the situation and realize the importance of the children staying in contact with the absent parent, they might encourage the children to write their parent while visiting with them or make an audio tape to send to their absent parent.

4. Realize that your child's self-esteem depends largely on being loved by *both* parents. While the custodial parent may be filling their heads with malicious misinformation about you, you can be sending them letters that at least let them know you are thinking of them and care. At a deep level children always know who really loves

and supports them. They aren't dumb, but it may take some time for them to put it all together.

5. If your time with your children is severely limited or nonexistent, keep a journal that will tell your children how much you miss them, as well as all your special thoughts about them. One woman, whose husband had taken her son and disappeared, began writing to express her deep hurt and longing for her child. She wrote him letters, including all the motherly wisdom she knew, even though her son never received them. Years later, she found him through relatives and was able to obtain court-ordered visitation rights. It took a while to break through his hostility because he felt she had abandoned him. When she thought he was ready, she showed him her journal, the returned letters, and the legal papers. It was quite a revelation for the son and an emotionally healing experience for both of them.

6. Make a conscious effort to comfort yourself with the knowledge that right is on your side. Having done all you can to contact your children and deal civilly with your ex-spouse, rest assured that you've done the right thing. Don't let visits turn into a grudge match, escalating the war between you and your ex-spouse, and don't descend to your ex-spouse's level. It may not feel good to turn the other cheek, but the children benefit tremendously.

7. Don't automatically assume that your ex-spouse is running you down in front of your children when they visit. When your children return and they act emotionally distant or alienated from you, realize that this is both natural and impossible to avoid. The other parent experienced it when the children arrived. After the non-custodial parent finally breaks through the children's emotional shells and reestablishes an emotional openness with them, it's probably time for the kids to go back home again. Most kids are overwhelmed by emotions too complicated for them to understand. They resent one par-

ent for leaving and don't want to love that person because of the pain inflicted on the family. Yet when they do give in to their feelings of love, they feel guilty. As they continue to rationalize something they don't understand, they are bombarded with anger, love, hate, pain, guilt, sadness, and a feeling of loss for what can never be. Of necessity, children build protective shells to keep the pain at a minimum. They think that if they don't love so much it won't hurt so much when the other person isn't there.

8. If you have a hostile ex-spouse or if *you* are a hostile ex-spouse, remember that the best interests of your children must come before your personal interests and desire for revenge. One six-year-old boy spoke for thousands of children when he said, ''I wish my mom and dad could talk to each other without fighting.'' Is that too much to ask? I urge you to consider what is best for your kids and put your personal animosities behind you when it comes to their welfare. In his book *Our Endangered Children, Growing Up in a Changing World*, social critic Vance Packard has outlined a ''Bill of Rights for Children of Divorce'' that we would all do well to follow.

1. Children of divorce are entitled to parents who set aside at least 20 minutes every month to discuss, in person or on the phone, the progress and problems of the children—and only the children. There should be no recriminations about any other topic, such as money. The children's schoolwork, health, mental state, activities, and apparent reaction to the divorce should be the focus of such talks.

2. Children of divorce are entitled to parents who go out to dinner together with them, if desired by the child, on their birthdays or on important holidays. The parents should also both go to school events important to the children.

3. Children of divorce are entitled to have parents who do not belittle the other parent in front of the children.

4. Children of divorce are entitled to have parents who refrain from any action that would seem to force the children to take sides.

5. Children of divorce are entitled to be free from any sense of pressure from either parent to serve as informants about the ex-partner's spending, dating, or other activities. If children freely choose to chat about the other parent, that is another matter.

6. Children of divorce are entitled to have complete freedom to phone either parent. If distances are involved, the calls will be collect. The children's parents will also agree that it is permissible for the non-custodial parent to call his or her children at least once a week.

7. Children of divorce are entitled to have parents who agree to notify each other in all emergencies or important events involving the children.

8. Children of divorce are entitled to have parents who by agreement are civil and avoid recriminations when they are in the presence of the child.[3]

When dealing with a hostile ex-spouse, all the adages about keeping a level head and maintaining your cool apply. Realize that your children didn't ask for all this trouble, and do what you can to keep them out of it. To keep a check on your own temper, follow the advice of Dr. Robert Eliot, a cardiologist: "Rule number one is don't sweat the small stuff. Rule number two is, it's all small stuff."[4]

| 12 |

I felt I didn't love my mother because I hated that she had left. When she calls to talk to me, my father has to force me to talk to her.

Ten-year-old boy

Communicating with Hostile Children

This section is almost an addendum to the last, since children who express hostility to the visiting parent have generally been well-trained by a hostile parent. Says Gardner:

On occasion a custodial parent may have such a distorted view of the absent parent that the term delusional becomes appropriate. A mother, for example, may expose the children to such continual vilification of their father that they come to fear and hate him, and may absolutely refuse to visit with him, even though ordered to by the court. The children may have been so "brainwashed" that they come to accept as valid their mother's delusion that their father is the incarnation of evil.[1]

The sheer hatred and animosity exhibited by one or two angry parents reaches its culmination here, having serious and lasting effects. The poison of hatred has worked its way into the children.

Gardner tells of one mother who so profoundly influenced her children that when their father arrived to pick them up for visits, they spat, cursed, and threw things at him. He had become the "embodiment of evil, filth, and treachery." Further attempts to contact the children were useless, of course, because even when messages got past the mother, the children had no desire to hear from him.

Despite this situation, we want to encourage you to keep communicating—be determined and unflagging in your efforts. The letters may go straight into the trash can, and the phone may be hung up repeatedly, but you're still doing some good. Gardner's advice to the father discussed above

> . . . was that he never stop completely from an occasional communication in order to reassure the children that he still loved them. I explained to him that the children's hatred (like his former wife's) revealed that affectionate feelings were still there, or else they would not have been so angry at him. Their anger revealed that they were still thinking about and were interested in him. To give up entirely might be considered by the children a rejection and would lessen the chances of their ever getting together again.[2]

Sometimes, after years of trying, the relationship between the non-custodial parent and children can be renewed as the children come to realize their absent parent was falsely maligned. The waiting is not easy, however.

Nicole lived with her mother and visited her father out of state every other holiday and six weeks during the summer. Although her father desperately wanted to have custody and never got it, Nicole's mother told her that her father deserted them both because he wanted to "be a free spirit, not tied down with a family." All phone calls and letters to Nicole were intercepted. When Nicole arrived for her court-ordered visits, she was generally full of anger and bitterness fueled by her mother's hostility. If she came for a week or two, she treated her father exactly like she had seen her mother treat him, like he was stupid and only existed to be put down.

In a very real sense, Nicole's father felt like it was his ex-wife that was visiting instead of Nicole because she looked and acted exactly like her mother. Their visits were frequently spent in arguments and tears. She would blame him for breaking up their family and making her life miserable, then tell him she hated him. Once Nicole got the pain and anger out of her system and had been away from her mother long enough, she would settle down and tell him she loved him.

Once she could relate to him as her father again, they would be very close for three days and have lots of long talks and good times. Then it was time for Nicole to leave again. Every time Nicole had to leave, her father cried unashamedly while getting her ready to return to her mother. Outwardly Nicole never cried in front of him, but her softened attitude toward him always turned to hardness once she went back to her mom. Maybe that was Nicole's way of coping with the pain. It was almost as though she taught herself to despise him and he had to break down the wall on each visit. If the visit was only for a weekend, it was always frustrating and full of anger because three days were never long enough to penetrate Nicole's shell.

Visitation can be very painful for a non-custodial parent as well as the child. Sometimes it is so emotionally wracking that the parent finds it easier to gradually withdraw rather than experience the reopening of the wounds each time. Often the children come laden with hostility and anger imposed upon them by the custodial parent. It may take a few hours or days for the noncustodial parent to break down the animosity and reestablish a relationship with the child. By the time that occurs, it's usually time for the child to leave. And once the children feel close to the parent again, they don't want to leave, and the parent has a hard time letting them go.

Parents should let the children know that they, too, are upset about the visit ending so soon, and they should always mention the *next visit*. The trauma of getting close then having to separate is difficult for both parent and child . . . maybe doubly so for the child. If the child comes home crying from having to leave the absent parent, he or she often thinks the custodial parent will feel betrayed or be angry.

Even if there is no open hostility between parents regarding visitation, the child often faces a lot of insecurities about being away from home, friends, and comfortable surroundings. If a third person was involved in the breakup of the marriage, it is important to allow the child as much time alone with the missing parent as possible, without the third party present. Even if the parent has remarried, this visitation time should center around the child and parent, not the new stepparent. Gradually bring in the new stepparent, but each visit should allow for some time alone between parent and child.

When the visit is over and it's time to go home, new emotional barriers are being built to cope with leaving again. These barriers often take the form of tears.

Robert was four when his father left his mother for another woman. During each visit Robert would throw temper tantrums and scream that he didn't want to go back home to his mother. He insisted that he wanted to live with his father. No amount of talking or reasoning with him would stop the crying. Although he was breaking his father's heart, his stepmother wondered if it wasn't a subtle attempt to force the stepmother to make them all go back home and live with their mother. For two years every visit was filled with screaming, yelling, and crying about how he wanted to live with his father. Gradually the crying and fits subsided as Robert realized the situation wasn't going to change and as he became more acclimated to his parents living separately.

Children can be master manipulators. Sometimes they believe that if they make it so miserable for the parents, they will force them back together, or so intolerable for the new stepparent that they can end the relationship.

Unfortunately, more often than not they are right. Various studies have shown that problems with stepchildren and ex-spouses are the number-one cause of the second marriage failing. However, it can backfire in some costly ways.

Margie was in high school when her father left her mother for another woman named Sarah. During her visits with her father, she determined to be as snotty and uncooperative as possible to her father's new wife. She always brought friends with her and encouraged them to be mean to Sarah. However, regardless of how mean everyone was to her, Sarah was consistently one of the nicest women you could meet, and Margie's dad dearly loved her.

Margie not only lost the battle but she lost the war. Over the years of insulting and cruel behavior toward Sarah, Margie found that she was less and less welcome in their home. The marriage has survived for thirty years now, but the father-daughter relationship has deteriorated to lunch once a year and a two-hour Christmas dinner. Who does Margie blame? The wicked stepmother, of course.

An important point to remember about hostile kids is that even in intact families kids also get hostile. Sometimes it is just their age and what is happening in their lives, rather than something concerning the divorce. If your children are in their teenage years and seem especially hostile toward you, it's best not to take it personally.

Most kids today face problems on a daily basis that were unheard of fifty years ago. The California Department of Education listed the top problems in the schools in 1940 as:

1. Talking
2. Chewing gum
3. Making noise
4. Running in the halls

5. Getting out of line
6. Wearing improper clothing
7. Not putting paper in the wastebaskets

The top problems in schools today are:

1. Drug abuse
2. Alcohol abuse
3. Pregnancy
4. Suicide
5. Rape
6. Robbery
7. Assault[3]

Teenagers face problems today that are far more serious than the problems we faced when we were their age. We had as many temptations, but most of the temptations had less serious consequences. Add these problems to the problems of a broken home . . . and the kids feel like there is nothing stable or dependable in their lives. Hostility toward their parents can be a very normal reaction.

In a recent discussion with Kelly Monroe, Assistant Chaplain of Harvard Graduate Christian Fellowship, she pointed out that besides these problems, "Today's children are exposed to more opportunities for self-destruction than ever before. And on top of that, they are given less wisdom and tools of self-discipline in public education than ever before. Today's teenagers are encouraged to lust after toys, cars, sex, clothes . . . an image imposed on them by those in the media who have discovered a multibillion-dollar market ready to be exploited.

"Parents, please remember that your children did not create this world of R-rated videos, purple hair, abusive language, drugs, and alcohol; it's an escape and a shield from the pressures and ugliness that surround them. It is strange logic that would blame the victim, and not the perpetrator. Those of us who have passively allowed the madness of this world to grow up around our children should not criticize them for living in it. Rather, we should lovingly rescue them, and ourselves, from it. Listen beneath the language of drug abuse, of sexual experimentation, of suicide, and hear the young people cry out. The cries beneath the words are for meaning, innocence, wonder, responsibility, purpose, beauty, home, love, and recognition. They long for what we held as true before our secular reasoning deceived us in another direction. And they will never have that until we adults demand it back, for ourselves, as well as for our children.''

To cope with the enormity of these problems kids need all the emotional support they can get from a stable home life and the love of an extended family. Unfortunately, during a divorce parents are so frequently consumed with their own problems they are unable to provide support to their children. When you add divorce to the kids' already monumental problems, it is often more than they think they can handle, especially teenagers . . . as witnessed by a rising suicide rate among teens.

Children and Teens Today magazine conducted a survey of their readership, which consists of ministers, lay counselors, administrators, therapists, and counselors who work with children and teens. They were asked, ''What do you see as the major stresses/problems facing today's teenagers?'' *Seventy-two percent* of the respondents listed ''problems arising from parental divorce/remarriage.''[4]

How long does the hostility and emotional trauma of divorce last? Expect long-term effects. Even after a reasonably civil divorce, many families still feel intense anger for many years.

If you find yourself in a hostile situation as the non-custodial parent, what can you do to make the most of every minute with your children?

- Use every conceivable occasion as an excuse to communicate with your child. Call or send them notes on holidays and special days when you are not going to be with them. Even Halloween . . . call and find out about their costumes, if they are going to parties, etc. After Halloween, call and ask them about their candy and if they had fun. Ask about school, tests, homework, sports, or dance class. Call them about any items of mutual interest, whether it is their favorite athletic team or a funny story you heard about a cat. Get a copy of their school calendar so you will know when they have days off and might possibly be home alone, and call them or try to arrange in advance to take them to lunch or have some form of contact with them. Avoid feeling rejected and don't stop trying.
- Realize how much your children's happiness and self-esteem depends on unconditional love from both parents. Children need more than your financial support. They need to know that you love them and want to see them even if you don't live with your ex-spouse any more.
- Don't worry if your children seem cold and indifferent to you. Realize that they may be poisoned against you by your ex-spouse and they have to let their minds sort through it all—which may take years.
- Remember, you might not be able to do anything about the hostility, lies, and anger directed toward you, but it won't last forever. Stay in there. Let your children know you love them. They won't always be little, though it seems that way now. Someday you will be able to relate to your children without all the garbage of interference by others. Hang on. It is worth it.

If your children have been trained to despise you, remember the words of the One who said, "Father, forgive them, for they do not know what they do."[5] Also remember, eventually "this too shall pass."

ACTIVITIES TO MAKE COMMUNICATION EASIER

Because of the tension often involved in visiting, sometimes it is difficult to get children to open up and start talking to you. Many children clam up when asked what is happening in school or with their friends. They may respond, "Nothing," or, "Just the same," and leave you wondering how to get a dialogue going.

Rather than carrying the entire weight of the conversation yourself, use some "Let's Pretend" questions. If your kids respond well to them, select one and carry it throughout the whole weekend or time you are together. These questions are not as threatening to children as direct questions, and can be a part of your visit regardless of whatever else you have planned—in fact, they may be the most productive thing you do together. When placed in the context of a game, they are more likely to solicit a response, revealing much about your children that you might not otherwise have found out. Try these in addition to any you think of on your own:

1. If you could have X-ray vision for just a few moments every day, when would you like to have it and how would you use it?

2. If you could travel in a time tunnel, where would you want to go and why?

3. If you could have any special power, what would you like it to be? How would you use it?

4. If you could change anything about yourself, what would it be? Why?

5. If you could do anything you are not allowed to do now, what would it be? Are you going to allow your children to do the things you can't do?

6. If you could make up all the rules you have to follow, what would your rules be?

7. If you could keep people from teasing you or saying anything about you that you don't like, what

kinds of things would you make them stop saying or teasing you about?

8. If your house caught on fire and you could only save what you could carry in one trip, what would you save? (Assume all the people and pets are safe outside.)

9. What would you do if everything only cost a penny? Where would you go? Who would you take with you?

10. If you could trade places with anyone in the world for just one day, who would you want to be? Why?

11. If you could not have your real mother and father, who would you want to be your mother and father. Why? (They don't have to have lived at the same time or be the same age.)

12. If you could be any other person who has ever lived, who would you want to be? Why? Where would you go and what would you do?

13. What is the best thing that has ever happened to you? Why? What is the best thing that happened to you since I last saw you? Why?

14. For just one week, if you could be any animal that ever lived in the world, what would you want to be and why?

15. If you could tell a child of divorce one thing to help them, what would you say?

16. If you could write a book that everyone in the world would read, what would you write about? Would you like to write a book? If so, why not start now by keeping a journal of ideas and thoughts?

If the children are interested, talk to your school or local librarian about books written by children. Trevor Ryan was ten years old when he wrote *What to Do When Mom and Dad Divorce* (Abingdon Press). S. E. Hinton was sixteen years old when she wrote *That Was Then,*

This Is Now, which became a very successful book and also a TV movie.

If the children like to talk about these topics, let them each design some questions that can be used. And they can be used any time—while driving, walking, sitting around, you name it. It can be a wonderful way to get your children to open up to you.

PRACTICE ACTIVE LISTENING

When children are venting their anger at you, do everything you can to control your tongue and practice active listening, which is simply feeding back to the other person what you thought they said to you. It is the practice of not getting angry, blaming, taking sides, or making subjective comments but rather reiterating the speaker's feelings. You neither agree nor disagree, but only reinforce the other's thoughts.

Active listening works especially well with hostile and angry children because it helps them bring their thoughts out into the open without lending confusion through inappropriate responses. The components of active listening are:[6]

1. Clarifying questions. These can help you better understand what your children are trying to say, and they can help them expand on the areas they need to explain further. Questions such as "What happened then?" or "How did you feel about that?" make the conversation flow more smoothly.

2. Paraphrasing. This *shows* the kids that you understand and gives them a chance to explain when you don't. "So you felt that kids were making fun of you because Mommy and Daddy are getting a divorce?" or "It sounds like that really made you feel bad" are ways to give feedback to your children as they are talking. Another way of paraphrasing is to look for patterns in the conversation—if your child keeps coming back to a certain point, bring that up: "You said that the kids laugh at you, your

teacher is being too hard on you, and I never listen. I think you feel like no one understands your problems.'' Comments like this can be a tremendous relief for a child; and, if you're not on target, they can show him or her what needs to be made clear.

3. Helping comments. These are the little words that keep someone talking: ''Uh-huh,'' ''Go on,'' ''Oh really?'' They simply serve to reassure your children that you *want* them to continue talking, as long as they are accompanied by eye contact.

Listen to a typical active listening conversation between Stevie, whose parents are getting a divorce, and his grandmother:

''Gee, Grandma, it's really tough around our house right now. Every time Mom and Dad get together they argue and fight and Dad slams the door and Mom breaks dishes and finally Dad takes off and drives real fast in the car. Mom just starts crying. I don't know what to do.''

''Sounds like you're pretty confused and scared, Stevie.''

''Yes, I really am. Last time I was afraid Dad was going to run into a big truck that was coming down the street. He was driving so fast and I know he was real upset.''

''You're really fearful for your father's life.''

''Yes, I don't know what he might do because I've seen him kind of lose control around the house, and maybe he would do something to hurt himself on purpose.''

''You sound real frightened now.''

''Yes, I don't know what to do about that because Mom cries and she goes in her room and shuts the door and sometimes I have to fix my own supper.''

''You're real worried about your mom, too, aren't you?''

''Yeah, I don't know what is going to happen if Dad finally moves out. I don't know if she can make it on her own, and I don't know what I'm going to do, either.''

"You're really worried about your future."
"Yeah, I really am."

These active listening techniques are great not only for hostile children and ex-spouses, but also when you are communicating on a positive level with your children or others.

In order to understand your child's feelings during this difficult time of divorce, you need to listen carefully to your children. Love your children and listen to them. When you think you are too busy or too exhausted to take time to talk to your children, remember the words and thoughts in this poem:

Listen to the Children

Take a moment to listen today
To what your children are trying to say

Listen today, whatever you do
Or they won't be there to listen to you

Listen to their problems, listen for their needs
Praise their smallest triumphs, praise their smallest deeds
Tolerate their chatter, amplify their laughter
Find out what's the matter, find out what they're after

But tell them that you love them, every single night
And though you scold them, make sure you hold them
And tell them "Everything's all right;
Tomorrow's looking bright!"

Take a moment to listen today
To what your children are trying to say
Listen today, whatever you do
And they will come back to listen to you!

                                        Denis and Susan Waitley[7]

13

Does Divorce Mean Discipline Problems?

I wish someone would tell my mom and dad my sister is playing games with them. If she doesn't get what she wants from Mom, she goes to Dad and stays there so she can get it.

Twelve-year-old boy

Laurie loved life and lived every moment to the fullest. Some people called her precocious, others said she was "a rascal," but everyone agreed life was never dull with Laurie around. She was nine when Linda and Bill, her parents, divorced. Linda's salary and child support were not enough to provide after-school care, so Laurie became a latch-key child. She was not allowed to cook, have friends over, or go outside until her mother got home, so she became quite creative in finding ways to entertain herself.

One afternoon Laurie decided to play "grown-up." She did her hair with Mom's heat rollers; put on Mom's best party dress, black stockings, and heels; and applied as much of Mom's makeup as would fit on her face. How wonderful she looked! But what fun was it if no one else could see her? Laurie decided it wouldn't hurt to invite Jennifer over to take a peek at her. She didn't see how her mother would find out as long as Jennifer was gone when she came home from work.

Jennifer loved the way Laurie looked and decided she wanted to dress up too. After Jennifer was suitably made up in Linda's other good dress, stockings, shoes, and makeup, the girls remembered that their favorite TV show was on. During the commercial Jennifer said she was hungry, so Laurie decided to cook something for her guest . . . after all, she had seen Mom do it many times. Bacon would be easy to fix, she thought, so she put the whole package in the skillet, poured in some cooking oil, and turned on the stove. As soon as their show came back on, they ran to watch it. During the next commercial they went into the bathroom to check on their makeup.

When Laurie's mother arrived home after a grueling day at the office, not to mention having to cope with inconvenient public transit schedules and worrying about how she and Laurie would survive, she opened the door and smoke came pouring out. Believing the apartment was on fire, she frantically screamed for Laurie. The bathroom door opened and out walked Jennifer and Laurie dressed in Linda's good clothes, which were now splattered with grease and makeup.

"Guess what, Mom! I made dinner for us," Laurie beamed.

Linda ran to the kitchen and found a bubbling skillet of grease, kitchen curtains decorated with dancing flames, and a very black pillar of smoke.

"Call 911!" Linda screamed as she turned off the stove and scrambled for a fire extinguisher.

After the fire fighters and Jennifer left, Linda realized how thankful she was that the girls were safe, but also how furious she was that once again Laurie had disobeyed her instructions.

Linda wondered: Is divorce synonymous with behavior problems? Why did she have so many behavior problems with Laurie? Couldn't she stay home alone without all these traumas? Do all divorced children act like this?

Children of divorce are frequently considered behavior problems by teachers, extended family, and friends. Bad behavior often gets shrugged off with a comment like: "What can you expect? Johnny is from a broken home."

WHY DO BEHAVIOR PROBLEMS
FREQUENTLY MULTIPLY AFTER A
DIVORCE?

It is more difficult to handle children during and after a divorce because both adults and children are experiencing many emotional ups and downs. Most frequently kids are angry, defiant, and heartbroken. One child said, "Divorce feels like my heart is a basketball and my parents are dribbling it all over the gym floor." When children can't control their emotions, it is very difficult for them to control their behavior.

Because of their fear of abandonment, they test their parents, often becoming angry and defiant to see how far they can go in manipulating or pushing their parents to the limit. During this difficult time in their lives, they need extra love, security, and attention—which neither parent may be emotionally capable of giving because they are having such a rough time stabilizing themselves.

Parents naturally find it harder to manage their children when their own emotions are bouncing off the wall. The changes involved in a divorce upset everyone's emotional equilibrium. Often it is easier to give in to the child than to withstand a barrage of endless crying, begging, pleading, or other manipulative techniques.

Prior to the divorce both parents probably handled discipline problems with one parent being firmer than the other. After the divorce they don't have a backup style or partner to take over when one is weak. If there were discipline problems in the home before the divorce, they will multiply afterwards.

Kids are also frequently subjected to two different sets of rules, or lack of rules, at each parent's home. If Mom has the kids most of the time, she may be so emotionally upset over the divorce and the added responsibilities of being a single parent that she is unable to be consistent in her discipline. Sometimes the kids can do anything they want, but the next time they do it, they are severely punished. Consistency may be difficult even before the divorce, but it is extremely important after the divorce.

If Dad is the non-custodial parent, he may find it very difficult to discipline the kids at all since he only sees them occasionally and has little quality time with them. His authority or influence over the children might be totally undermined by derogatory comments the mother makes to the children about their father, causing them to lose respect for him. Permissiveness may prevail during visitation times until the behavior is so out of control that visits are cut short. Generally, it takes extra effort from Mom to discipline the kids when they come home from Dad's house.

If a stepparent enters the picture and tries to get involved in disciplining the children, the kids may resent it so much that they deliberately misbehave to cause problems in the home. Various studies reveal that the biggest troublemakers in first marriages are money and sex. But most problems in remarriages center on how to raise and discipline children.[1]

Divorce is traumatic for both parents and children, but it does not automatically mean that your children will be out of control. One of the greatest things you can do for them is to teach them to be well-behaved and to respect others. The way to do this is to set limits and discipline them with love. Always distinguish between loving children and not accepting their behavior. Let your kids know that their misbehavior does not restrict your love, but that you discipline them because you love them.

WHAT IS THE GOAL OF DISCIPLINE?

The goal of good discipline is for children to obtain inner convictions that will prevent objectionable and destructive behavior. Until children develop internal controls themselves, it is necessary for parents to practice external controls. Also, we want to extinguish negative behavior and replace it with positive, healthy behavior—otherwise it is too one-sided.

WHY IS DISCIPLINE SO IMPORTANT?

Discipline is the seed of freedom. Unless children learn responsibility and self-discipline, they will never develop fully in life and learn how to become truly independent emotionally or economically.

WHAT DOES DISCIPLINE TEACH CHILDREN?

When discipline is handled correctly, it teaches children to do the right thing without being told and gives them a sense of control over their own behavior. If children are given consistent, strong boundaries or limitations, their self-worth grows as they abide by these guidelines and realize they are capable of managing their own life situations.

DOES DISCIPLINE HELP DEVELOP A CHILD'S CONSCIENCE?

Good discipline teaches a child more than the fact that certain behaviors bring certain responses. It should develop a child's conscience by teaching him or her to think about and learn the difference in right and wrong behavior for any given situation.

Children should learn to do what is right because of the good feeling it gives them to behave. If children do not abide by the standards they know to be appropriate, they feel a loss of self-esteem from their own lack of ability to act accordingly. Self-worth is directly related to abiding by morals, standards, values, and behavior we know to be appropriate.

WHAT IS THE DIFFERENCE BETWEEN DISCIPLINE AND PUNISHMENT?

Discipline involves setting limits or boundaries for the child, stating in advance the consequences of breaking the rules, and enforcing them consistently. It can include positive and negative reinforcement, although positive reinforcement produces more of the desired results.

Punishment is a spontaneous emotional reaction to misbehavior that only relieves the parent's anger. This may include striking, hitting, slapping, or spanking the child before all the facts are known. It can also include withdrawing privileges or invoking certain sanctions on the child's behavior. The key point is that it is done in the heat of emotion rather than by considering what is appropriate. If screaming and yelling were involved on the part of the parent, the parent was not in control. Punishment is detrimental to children and damages the parent-child relationship. It may extinguish the negative behavior temporarily, but at the cost of self-esteem and the likelihood that the negative behavior will reappear.

CAN DISCIPLINE EVER BE HARMFUL TO A CHILD?

Discipline that does not teach self-control can be very damaging. Behavior will be repeated. Avoid discipline that only imposes external controls. When a child's behavior is controlled by an authority figure, the good behavior usually only lasts as long as the authority is present.

When attempting to control your children's actions or behavior, you must be very careful not to break their spirits. Children's spirits, or attitudes and feelings about themselves, are directly related to their personal worth and self-esteem.

Sometimes the discipline itself is the cause of a child's poor behavior. Although it is only natural to do so, don't repeat the same mistakes your parents made with you. If you do spank your children, never hit them any place except on their covered bottom with one swat.

WHAT ARE SOME THINGS I SHOULD NEVER DO IN DISCIPLINING MY CHILD?

Don't ridicule, embarrass, belittle, insult, shame, or humiliate your children with verbal assaults, especially in front of others. After a divorce children are extremely fragile and need to be built up rather than torn down.

Don't withdraw your love when they misbehave. By saying, "If you do that, Mommy won't love you anymore," you make them feel their personal worth is conditional upon approved behavior. If Dad has just moved out of the home, the child's greatest fear is that Mommy is going to leave too. Withdrawing your love can undermine all their security.

Don't discipline for mistakes or clumsy behavior. They should clean up the milk they spilled rather than be spanked for it. One of the positive aspects of divorce is that afterwards children generally learn to accept more responsibility because of the missing parent in the home. Don't do anything for them that they can do for themselves.

Don't let your emotional state determine your discipline. If you are upset, don't take it out on the kids. When you hear your kids say, "Watch out, Mom's had a bad day," you can be reasonably sure you have done this in the past. After a physically and emotionally exhausting day it is easier to shut out the kids and let them get away with bad behavior than to pull yourself together enough to deal with them. Sometimes you feel like saying, "I don't care what you do, just don't kill each other," and retreating to your room. Kids realize this and can be very manipulative. Try to be consistent in which behaviors are acceptable and which ones will invoke restrictions. Things shouldn't be OK one day and punishable the next—depending only upon your mood. Children need firm and consistent boundaries and guidelines after a divorce. It is part of the stability only you can provide.

Don't discipline your kids when you are angry. You will say or do something you later regret. Wait until you cool down. Remember, everyone's emotions are raw now. At some level, parents may blame their kids for the divorce. It can be devastating to a child if in a fit of anger you scream at them, "If you kids didn't fight all the time, your dad never would have left home."

Don't say: "You make me angry." Say, "When you act this way, I feel angry." When you try to blame the children for your anger, they will feel bad about themselves and think that if they are the reason for your anger, they must also be the reason for your tears of sadness, your depression, and probably also the divorce. This is very damaging.

Don't say: "You treat me just like your father (or mother) did," or, "You're just like your father (or mother)!" More than likely something your children will do will remind you of your ex-spouse. It might be a put-down or a clumsy behavior. When that happens, be careful you don't say things to your kids that you really want to express to your ex-spouse. If you punish them on the grounds that their actions are like those of their absent father or mother, it shows disapproval toward their missing parent and is a double insult to them.

Don't argue with your kids or resort to screaming, yelling, or nagging. It becomes a meaningless habit rather than a way to get action. Also, it puts you on their level. Everyone is going to be more argumentative after the divorce because of all the changes, the uncertainties, and the unresolved emotions of anger, hurt, and grief. Realize this, try to be more tolerant, and neutralize situations before they get out of hand.

Don't imply that your children are a burden to you or that they weren't wanted in the first place. Financially and emotionally you might at times consider your children as burdens during the struggle to survive after a divorce, but money cannot buy the wonderful love and enjoyment your children can give you. Be careful not to complain about their financial needs in front of them, and never tell them their father doesn't give you enough money. Instead, look for creative and innovative ways to meet their needs as well as your own, and find happiness in the non-material aspects of life.

Don't discipline your children for something they didn't do or fall into the trap of disciplining all your kids for the misbehavior of one. Give them the benefit of the doubt. This is a common trap single parents fall into. Prior to the divorce most couples shared in the discipline. Afterward it is easier to lump everyone together rather than give the situation the time and attention it needs to isolate the guilty party. Think about the times during your own childhood when you were punished for something you didn't do. How did you feel about it? It is better to let the guilty party go unpunished and live with his or her own guilt than to punish an innocent party and have him or her live with resentments.

Don't discipline your children by withholding something they are entitled to—like meals. This might seem like an archaic punishment out of a TV show in the '50s, but some parents still do punish kids by saying, "Because you were a bad boy you have to go to bed without supper." After a divorce, children of all ages worry about having their basic needs met. They wonder, "Who will feed me and take care of me? If Daddy left, will Mommy leave too? If Mommy says she doesn't have enough money, will this mean I won't get to eat?" If you are too tired to fix a meal, don't look for an excuse for taking a meal away from them as punishment. Don't risk damaging their sense of security over having their basic needs met by taking away something they need. Children need the stability and security of food, clothing, shelter, love, and appropriate discipline. However, there is nothing wrong with teaching them about consequences. If you announce that dinner will be at 6:00 and John doesn't come home until 7:30, he will have the natural consequence of warming up his own food.

Don't be unreasonable about withholding special priv ileges—such as birthday parties or fun celebrations—for punishment. It is terribly damaging to a child's self-esteem to be punished by not being allowed to join in the celebration of a special occasion because of a behavior infraction. Parents who do this try to get their own power needs met by imposing unfair sanctions on their children. Unfortunately, after a divorce the party who was left often feels so helpless that he or she tries to regain power by invoking unreasonable behavior demands upon his or her children. Likewise, the parent who left may be so filled with bitterness over losing control of the family home and the children that his or her only method of achieving control is by trying to use power plays in dealing with the ex-spouse and children.

Don't treat your children as though their explanations, alibis, or opinions aren't worth anything, or they will feel like second-class citizens. Give them a chance to tell their side of the story.

Most frequently parents do not agree on discipline matters before a divorce. After a divorce there is even less agreement. At Dad's house, for instance, certain behaviors might be allowed, accepted, and even encouraged, but they may be forbidden at Mom's house. Jumping on the bed is one example. When they can do it at Dad's house (which might be a rented, furnished apartment), they are going to try it at Mom's house. Children might actually feel that since Dad allowed it, it is a permissible activity now. Ask them why they violated your rule. If they say, "Because Daddy lets us," you need to explain some things to them rather than punish them for it. Tell them that when they are at Dad's house they can follow Dad's rules, but when they are at Mom's house, they follow Mom's rules.

Don't expect your children to be perfectly self-controlled . . . if they were, they wouldn't be normal. Realize that some misbehavior is unrelated to the divorce and is just a natural part of childhood. However, many children do act out their feelings about the divorce in the form of misbehavior and might be using it as a ploy to draw Mom and Dad back together. If they constantly get in trouble at school, it could be because both Mom and Dad have to go see the principal together, and the children hope it will result in Dad coming back home.

14

Making Discipline More Effective

Just as being the perfect child is abnormal, so is being the perfect parent. We all make mistakes. The good news is we can recover from those mistakes, most of the time.
Jane Nelson, author of *Positive Discipline*

Experiences with my children taught me that there is an exception to every rule and rules exist to be broken. But if you only remember one guideline, remember this: Teaching obedience should never be at the expense of a loving relationship with your child.

HOW TO DISCIPLINE WITH LOVE

1. Set boundaries, guidelines, or limits, and let your children know what they are. Also let them know the consequences of exceeding those limits.

Boundaries are generally handled in one of these ways:

- Children aren't given any boundaries. If a parent says, "You can do anything you want. I trust your judgment," or "I give up, just go do it, I can't do anything with you any more," the child will probably feel very confused and possibly unloved. That is a "no boundary" kind of family. Children want and need some behavioral guidelines—whether or not they choose to follow them.
- Children are given a boundary so solid that no love can come through. Authoritarian parents are often so strict,

123

and structure the child's boundaries so rigidly, that the child does not feel loved. If children aren't told the logic behind the rules, they often feel the rules are an attempt to prevent them from having a good time. When the consequences of violating the boundaries are so rigid the parent doesn't even listen to the child's explanation, the child might become frustrated and intentionally violate boundaries that might not have been crossed otherwise.

• Children are given inconsistent boundaries. Unfortunately, this is the most common method practiced by parents. Sometimes certain behaviors are permissible and other times they aren't. Sometimes children feel loved and accepted and other times they don't. That creates confusion. Also, if a child can do something one time and the next time gets punished for it, the child may feel loved one time and unloved the next. This is frequently the way children feel when Dad allows them to do certain things at his house but the same activities are forbidden at Mom's.

• Children are given consistent love with consistent boundaries. This is the preferred method. The child always knows what behaviors are allowed and which ones are prohibited. At an appropriate age level the parents give their children an explanation for each boundary they question. This child experiences consistent, predictable, and appropriate love and discipline in his or her life.

2. Try environmental control by substituting the items they are fighting over for another article, or prohibit them from participating in an activity they enjoy, or change their location. Use isolation for small periods of time. But *never* punish your children, your ex-spouse, or the grandparents by withholding visitation privileges.

One technique that is especially effective with small children, but can only work up to around age ten, is called "Time Out." William Glasser, originator of reality therapy, was one of the first innovative educators to use "Time Out" in schools. His purpose was not to punish but to give students the opportunity to take "time out" to see if their behavior was getting them what they wanted. You might tailor make this approach to your child at home by the following method: Tell your kids before they misbehave that the next time they do something unacceptable, they have to go right to their room (or other designated area) and stay in there for fifteen minutes. Tell them they can come out only if they haven't argued about going to their room. If they have argued, require them to stay there for an additional fifteen minutes.

When using this technique, don't lecture or tell your children how bad they are. If you say, "You knew this was going to happen," or "You shouldn't have done that," it is like feeding candy to them . . . they get the attention they want.

At the end of the fifteen minutes, if they haven't screamed or yelled or argued, open the door and tell them they can come out. Although this doesn't sound like a big deal to an adult, when a child has to go to his or her room and doesn't get any attention—positive or negative—it's not fun. For very small children five minutes is probably sufficient. After a divorce children need considerably more attention than before, so this form of discipline is really effective for them.

3. Try to prevent misbehavior with democratic discipline. Giving children a voice in their own government teaches responsibility and self-reliance, and it encourages mental and emotional growth, creativity, and a strong self-concept. You can only teach responsibility by giving responsibility.

As soon as possible, let your children participate in the rules they must abide by and in the punishment for breaking them. That way the rules will have more meaning. Allow your kids to have a say in what their punishment should be. Sharing power with children is only possible if you have high self-esteem.

Susan's twelve-year-old son, Mark, became very angry, rebellious, and arrogant during his parents' divorce. His father left his mother for another woman, but Mark often blamed his mother for his father's departure. He also wondered if his father loved him.

One of the things that irritated and hurt Susan the most was when he made derogatory remarks, sassed, or talked back to her. This was more than Mark expressing a difference of opinion; it was outright defiance and disrespect. Sometimes she would discipline him for it, and other times she would just yell at him and tear him down for it, depending upon her emotional strength at the time.

Since his father left, all Mark wanted to do was watch TV, play video games, or listen to his stereo. Susan finally sat down and negotiated with him, telling him she did not appreciate it when he talked like that to her and she didn't like herself when she screamed at him. She asked him to work with her on a suitable punishment that would make him reconsider before he talked back and would prevent her from saying things she would later regret.

After a few minutes they agreed that if Mark talked back, he could not watch TV for twenty-four hours. Susan would turn off the TV and write down the time with a note that said, "No TV for twenty-four hours." Three different times Mark talked back, and Susan was consistent in leaving the TV off for twenty-four hours. It worked so well that by the third time Mark came to his mom and asked her if they could do something together.

This simple technique resulted in a breakthrough in their relationship. They started cooking and baking things together. They also visited bookstores and libraries and found books that interested Mark. They began to relate on a different level. Mark was able to get positive attention from his mother, and he no longer felt a need to challenge her. Susan was filling part of the void left by his father's departure.

4. Teach responsibility by letting children experience

the unfortunate consequences of their actions—but not in life-threatening situations.

After Mike's parents divorced he started attending a private school, which he claimed to love. Two months later, after numerous conferences with the parents, the school officials asked Mike's parents to withdraw him from the school because they were unable to control his behavior. Mike continually started fights with the other kids, insulted his teacher, and refused to follow her instructions.

Mike was put in another private school, but they tolerated his behavior less than a month. Each day he was sent to the principal, who had to call his parents to come to the school and tell them about Mike's latest actions. Same verdict: Mike is uncontrollable and we do not want him in our school.

Enrollment in a public school came next. After one week Mike was suspended for kicking his teacher and spitting on her when she corrected his behavior. Mike's behavior was out of control. The incredible part of this true story is that Mike was only six years old and in the first grade.

Prior to the divorce, Mike was energetic and aggressive, but he did not display hostile behavior to others. However, the physical fights and venom spit out between his parents frightened Mike and made him angry.

Mike cried because he wanted to go back to school. Everyone tried to explain that if he fought and talked bad to the teacher, he could not stay in school. Mike was experiencing the unfortunate consequences of his actions. So were his parents.

When one parent insults and denigrates the other parent in front of the children, it has a devastating effect on their lives and value systems. One little girl said, "I know my dad can't be as bad as Mom says he is." Mike said, "If Mom is as bad as Dad says she is, my teachers must be bad too." His behavior toward his teachers was similar to what he had witnessed between his parents.

Parents need to realize the consequences of their own behavior and help their children to do the same.

5. Commend and reinforce good behavior. Encourage desired activities and try ignoring negative actions. Look for signs of progress.

After giving Mike a series of psychological and aptitude tests, his counselor discovered that he had an exceptionally high IQ, and more than likely, his classroom situation offered insufficient challenge. When Mike came back to school he was placed in the gifted program with the understanding that he could stay in school only if he didn't fight and did what his teacher told him to do. Mike was also allowed to work on a computer for an hour a day if the rest of his classroom work was finished. He became totally consumed and fascinated by the computer and begged to work on it all day long.

Mike demanded, wheedled, cried, and begged his father to buy him a computer that he could work on at home. After three hours of Mike attempting every conceivable manipulation to obtain his computer, his dad came up with an ingenious idea. He promised Mike that if he could go all week without getting in trouble at school, on the weekend they would go shop for computers, try them out, and look for one suitable to his age. But he wouldn't buy it unless Mike finished the school year without getting suspended again. And each week Mike was good, his dad would arrange for him to have some time on a computer.

Mike agreed to the plan. His dad found a computer time-sharing store with facilities for children. Each week Mike made it through without his dad or mom being called to the school, Mike was allowed one to three hours in the computer store to work and play on the computer. The fee for using the computer was minuscule compared to taking time off work to handle his behavior problems.

By the end of the school year Mike was a different kid. He told his teacher and all his friends his behavior had improved, so he could get a computer. Mike's dad found a kid's computer for around one hundred dollars that offered sufficient challenge to Mike. However, he showed him what each of the more expensive models could do that his computer couldn't. He assured Mike that if he continued to behave and learned how to use his computer, he would buy him the other computers as he grew older.

Mike's behavior was changed by giving him positive reinforcement. Dad is working on his behavior with the help of a counselor. The counselor is trying to convince him how damaging it is to insult Mike's mother in front of their son.

6. Help your children save face when embarrassed, and be careful to maintain their integrity.

If your children take something from a store, go back to the store with them to return the item. Don't allow them to merely return the item to the counter. Ask to speak to the manager, explain what they did, and have them say they are sorry and that it will never happen again. Take as much responsibility for the incident as your children do. Many young children do occasionally pick up an item when shopping with their parent and leave the store without telling the parent about it. However, if this happens more than once or twice, or after your child is old enough to realize this is wrong behavior, you need to take a more serious look at it.

Statistically, many children resort to petty theft or other forms of delinquency after a divorce. For some it may be an attempt to get their parents' attention, while for others it may be symptomatic of unresolved anger or resentment. If your child is headed down this road, seek professional help immediately.

7. Spend time with your children. A high correlation exists between parental involvement and a child's behavior and adjustment. Many problems are just a desire for attention. All behavior is an attempt to get our needs met. When your children start misbehaving, ask yourself what needs they are trying to meet.

One fifteen-year-old boy wrote, "I want to be spoiled at Dad's so I fake being sick. It's the only time I get attention."

Although this child pretended to be sick to get attention, many other children find the only way they can get any attention from their mother or father is by getting in trouble. After a divorce, children need extra comfort and reassurance of your love and affection. Investing time in your children's lives may save you many hours of misery as a result of misbehavior or delinquency.

8. Make sure the punishment is related to the misbehavior, or your kids will learn nothing.

Barry, age nine, was caught taking ice-cream bars from a neighbor's freezer.

After his mother, Barbara, reprimanded him, he said, "I haven't been eating them, honest!"

"What have you been doing with them?" Barbara asked.

"Selling them to my friends for a quarter each. They have to pay a dollar if they buy them from the ice-cream truck. I thought it was a good way to earn money."

Rather than grounding Barry and making him pay for the ice cream he stole, Barry and his mother worked out a repayment plan. Barry apologized to the neighbor and agreed to do chores for her after school for an hour a day until the debt was paid off. After he paid off his debt, the neighbor asked him to come over twice a week and do chores for her—for which he was paid.

9. Have reasonable expectations for your children's behavior. Remember, making mistakes is a part of learning. Make special allowance for their behavior during the divorce and other stressful times. We all have good days and bad days. Work on increasing the number of good days.

10. Admit your mistakes. No one is perfect. Recognize that no one can be right all the time or wrong all the time. If you can admit you are wrong, your children will also be willing to admit when they are wrong. Your chil-

dren will overlook your mistakes if they sense an underlying feeling of love.

Believe in your children. Show them you trust them. If others accuse your child of some wrongdoing, get your child's version of the story and carefully consider whether or not the other side may be distorting the facts for their own purposes—even if the accusing party is an adult. Someone said it is better to let a guilty man go free than to sentence an innocent man to death. Although discipline matters aren't that extreme, the same principle applies. Give your children every benefit of the doubt that they are telling you the truth.

11. Seek to support your children rather than discourage them. Respect their feelings. A large part of your child's self-worth comes from your attitude toward him or her. Seek ways to meet your needs and your child's needs. Build your own self-esteem and help your children develop theirs. Find ways to grow together.

12. Encourage independence and competence. Give children room to grow. Respect their need for freedom. Children are generally not allowed to choose which parent they want to live with until they are at least fourteen years of age. However, some parents allow children the freedom to choose, independent of the court ruling.

Tim and Carol were only sixteen when they married after Carol became pregnant. Fortunately, they were able to maintain a good friendship after the divorce and both wanted what was best for their daughter, Cynthia. Although Carol and Cynthia moved two thousand miles away from Tim, they maintained a good strong relationship for ten years with both Tim and his parents. Cynthia never was a behavior problem, but Carol always allowed her to make her own decisions and felt she made the right choices.

When Carol asked Cynthia what she wanted for her thirteenth birthday, she said, "I really want to get to know my dad by living with him in Arizona for a year."

Everyone involved was surprised, but Carol wisely decided to allow Cynthia her freedom of choice.

Cynthia and her father had a wonderful year together getting to know each other at a very sensitive time in her life. Both Carol and Tim had confidence in Cynthia and allowed her room to grow in an area that had previously been restricted by the divorce. The cooperation between the parents minimized behavior problems with Cynthia.

13. Laugh with your children and at yourself. Let the atmosphere be one of friendliness and cooperation. Although most custodial parents are mothers, and we frequently hear about their problems running the household, ten percent of the custodial parents are fathers and they, too, have many problems adapting to increased household responsibilities. Movies such as *Kramer vs. Kramer* and *Mr. Mom* give us insight into problems that some men have in developing their housekeeping skills.

Tom was a successful businessman and owner of his own company when he divorced and obtained custody of his two children, ages ten and twelve. For the first time in his life, Tom found himself trying to prepare meals because the children did not like to go out to eat and he did not like fast food. Each day was a new challenge. Somewhat embarrassed, he started hanging around the lunchroom at noon asking various women in his company for easy recipes and cooking tips. Everyone started bringing him recipes, complete with detailed instructions and a list of the ingredients so he could go right home and start cooking.

Every day he would come back to the office and tell the women what happened and how his meal turned out. The children would come by after school for a ride home, and they would tell their version of the meal too. Mealtimes turned into a hilarious recital of Dad's culinary attempts. After a couple of weeks he started assigning responsibilities, and each of the children was responsible for a meal.

They all grew together through the divorce and Mom's

absence from the home. It was obvious to the kids that Dad was doing everything possible for them, and they all had a good time developing their survival skills. Behavior problems were at a minimum in this home where love and laughter abounded.

14. Love your children enough to make them mind. Treat them with love and respect, and discipline them with love and respect. Your goal is to change their actions—not put them down or change their personalities. Help them maintain their dignity by giving them emotional support, consistent love, attention, and affection. We've said it before, and we'll say it again: children need additional love during and after a divorce. Tell them often that you love them. Show your love by being affectionate, giving them as much of your time as possible, listening to them, and doing things with them. Most important of all, always restore the love relationship after discipline.

ANYTHING ELSE I SHOULD REMEMBER?

Yes. Negative behavior is the child's way of telling us something is wrong in his or her life.

Until both parents and children adjust to the divorce, you can expect some form of behavior problems in children. To make that adjustment easier, it is important that you:

- *Do not* criticize or degrade the absent parent.
- *Do not* allow your relatives or friends to put down the child's absent parent in front of the child.
- *Provide* structure and routine for your children. They need the stability of knowing what they are supposed to do and not do, and when they are to do it or not do it.
- *Give* children added responsibilities equal to their abilities. Meeting these commitments increases their feelings of worth.
- *Establish* consistent guidelines for their behavior and

enforce them. Children want and need discipline. It
assures them that you love them.
* *Prevent* behavior problems by helping children feel
good about themselves and confident of your love.

Also remember that children model their behavior after adults. Little girls talk to their dolls the way their
mother talks to them. Frequently children treat their parents the way their parents treated them or the way they
see their parents treat their grandparents. Is your own
behavior part of your child's behavior problems? If so,
consider seeking outside help from friends or a counselor
to work on your own area of need.

Many children who grow up in a religious atmosphere
turn self-righteous during a divorce and will preach at
the parent they consider the sinner. Peggy was thirteen
years old when Jeannie, her mother, left her father, Da-
vid, for another man. Very frequently when Jeannie
would reprimand Peggy for her behavior, Peggy would
preach to her mother and say, "The Bible says divorce
is a sin. Why are you telling me I shouldn't have sex
before I am married when you are committing adul-
tery?"

Children will be the first to point out inconsistencies
they see in their parents' lives and feel fully justified in
either acting self-righteously about their own behavior or
in modeling their behavior after their parents. It is very
difficult to teach your children appropriate behavior if
you say, "Do as I say, not as I do."

Discipline begins with the parents and ends when the
children adopt and practice their own standards of right
and wrong. If you don't have it all together, you can't
expect to show your children how to behave. The key to
your children's behavior is your response to their behavior. When you take responsibility for your behavior, your
children will take responsibility for theirs too. If your
behavior is out of control, more than likely your children's behavior will be out of control. Consider joining

one of the wide variety of support groups that are available to assist in particular behavior problems. Read some of the self-help books that are available and offer assistance in many different types of behavioral problems. Contact your local mental health organization or hospital for referrals for a counselor or therapist.

You can't really change anyone else's behavior. You can only change your own behavior. But when you change, other people may change in their reaction to you.

15

Protecting and Nurturing Your Child's Self-Esteem

A child's life is like a piece of paper on which every passerby leaves a mark.

Chinese proverb

The little girl who is beaten will beat her doll baby.

Russian proverb

For hundreds of years women in China bound their young daughters' feet in order to hinder their growth. Although it was extremely painful and caused terrible deformity, mothers continued this practice throughout the growing years because tiny feet and a dainty walk were considered very feminine and the only way a young woman could hope to marry.

These same mothers had horrible childhood memories of the excruciating agony they had experienced and how they cried out for relief. But when they grew up, married, and had daughters of their own, the crippled mothers would get out the bindings and wrap their own daughters' feet, creating a new generation of crippled women.

Numerous studies reveal that we have a tendency to treat our own children as we were treated—the bad as well as the good. The very things we detested about our own parents are the things we find ourselves doing to our children.

Much like customs that are passed down from one generation to the next, our ability to raise children with high self-esteem depends upon our ability to develop and maintain high self-esteem ourselves. If we have low self-esteem, chances are that our children will have low self-esteem too; because we perceive and treat our children as we perceive and treat ourselves. If we devalue ourselves we devalue our children. It's that simple. Children of divorce have a hard time feeling good about themselves, they need our assistance.

Divorce is one of the most negative marks that can be made on children because it knocks the emotional props right out from under them. But parents can take tangible, positive steps to minimize the damage of divorce and make it a growing experience for their children. What are some of the things we can do to protect and nurture a child's self-esteem?

PROVIDE UNCONDITIONAL LOVE

One of the best ways you can help your children survive a divorce is to show them that they are unconditionally loved. This kind of love is based not on the way they behave, but on who they are—their simple existence. Even though you may feel unconditional love for your children, they may not know it from what you say. This is because children sometimes have trouble distinguishing themselves from their behavior.

If you say, "You spilled Mommy's perfume; you're a bad boy," your child may not understand that spilling Mommy's perfume is bad, but instead believe that he or she is bad. Children are dependent on their parents for survival itself, so the idea of rejection is terrifying.

Some of the things parents can say to children—or to themselves—to help them feel wanted and loved include: "I'm glad you're here—I love you very much," "I like to be with you," "You make me happy by being just like you are."

This gives children a sense of worthiness. Also, it assures them that the divorce was not their fault. Love is the most important contribution a parent can make toward a child's self-esteem. It is essential to be warm and emotionally involved in their lives.

BE GENEROUS WITH TOUCH

Another way of showing children love is through physical contact. During a divorce, children may feel extremely lonely. They often lose a sense of relatedness, not only to their families, but to the world in general. Children of all ages need to be touched; a hug, a kiss, or just holding hands all communicate affection. Of course different children want and need different amounts of physical attention, and a child who is not used to being touched may be suspicious and standoffish at first. A squeeze on the shoulder or a gentle pat on the back may be a more subtle way to communicate affection without making the child uncomfortable.

Touching is a form of nonverbal communication, as are body language and facial expressions. If you tell a child, "I love you," but your arms are crossed and your eyes look away, the child tends to hear the nonverbal message more clearly. Eye contact and an open, relaxed position, leaning toward the child rather than away, show that you are interested.

TEACH YOUR CHILD IT'S OK TO LOVE BOTH PARENTS

Children need to give and receive love from both parents. If children feel caught between their mother and father, feeling that to love one is to betray the other, they are in a no-win situation—and serious damage to their self-esteem may result.

Each parent has the opportunity to nurture their children's self-esteem by stressing that they can give and receive love from *both* parents. Make sure they understand that by giving love to one, they do not take love away from another. Give your children love and affection, and encourage them to express their love for you—don't be too busy for a hug.

PLACE NO CONDITIONS ON WHO THEY LOVE

Children need the love of an extended family—from their mother's and their father's sides. Help your children maintain good relationships with the extended family of both parents, whether or not they are being cordial to you. A loving support group provides strength and continuity throughout a child's life. Everything else may seem uncertain, but love is there as an anchor. It is a sustaining comfort. And your children's concept and definition of love are formed by their interaction with their parents and extended family. Children need to know they can always count on the love and support of special people regardless of whether these people love each other.

GIVE YOUR CHILD VERBAL AFFIRMATION

Praising a child is an obvious method of building self-esteem, but some methods of praise work better than others. Saying, ''You're a good kid,'' makes children feel good about themselves, but more specific praise, such as ''You've been really cooperative today,'' shows you have really noticed them.

It is important to praise not only the things your children succeed in but also the efforts they make. If they cleaned their rooms for the first time and botched the job, you can still say, ''I like the way you work on doing things for yourself,'' rather than saying, ''What a lousy job!'' When they work hard at something they aren't naturally good at, praise can especially boost self-esteem in a shaky area and show them that trying new things is rewarding rather than just frightening.

In general, children have fewer ways than adults to know how they're doing in *any* area; whether they are succeeding or failing, whether there is any point in continuing the effort. We all look to outside sources in order to monitor our own behavior, but adults tend to have more internal reference points; children have fewer experiences to compare with their present situations.

Lots of things are changing your children's lives now; they may be enrolled in a new school, taking on new responsibilities at home, and maybe even coping with new house rules. They need you to tell them where they need to improve and where they are doing well. If they have been making an effort or improving and no one notices, they may conclude that there is no point in trying. Yet it is easy to tell a child, "I know you've been trying real hard to get along with your sister . . . do more housework . . . or get better grades." All a parent has to do is *notice*.

MAKE SURE YOUR PRAISE IS SINCERE

Not all compliments, however, are good for children's self-esteem. Compliments that are exaggerated or over-generalized—"You always get such good grades," "Mommy's little girl always looks like a princess!" "My boy never spills any food"—tend to make children feel that they are either operating under false premises, or that you are lying to make them feel better about something they really do "badly." If children sometimes get bad grades or spill their food, they will be uneasy that you will find this out and withdraw your approval. If they have not as yet "spoiled" the compliment by making a mistake, they may live in continual anxiety, believing that you expect them to be perfect.

In fact, in order to have good self-esteem, children need negative as well as positive feedback for the same reasons: they need to know that you see when they make mistakes and that you still accept them and are willing to help them.

DEVELOP A SENSE OF BELONGING

Children need to feel wanted and loved by their family members, but they also need a sense of belonging. In a family that has split up, the children may not know where they belong, whether they are wanted, needed, or loved. They may also lose important role models when one parent leaves the family and feel a loss of control in their life—leaving them feeling helpless and victimized.

This sense of belonging is tied to places and things as well. Your children's sense of identity can be strengthened by the bonds they feel with the place they live and their own room.

Parents need to make sure that their children's sense of belonging does not depend entirely on places or things; yet they do need to recognize that their children need a place to call their own and objects that are familiar and reassuring. Just these efforts alone can do much to make children feel good about themselves, especially when many things may seem new and different.

Objects in particular can make the child feel secure. For example, a favorite blanket, toy, or gift given to children by their absent parent may have particular significance; and they may be able to express feelings about the parent using the object as a sounding board. Objects frequently have special, "magic" meanings to a child, and parents can encourage this use of symbolism and imagination.

When Sarah was born, someone special to her mother gave her a flower arrangement in a music box shaped like a baby's cradle. From the day she came home from the hospital, Sarah's mother wound up the music box and put Sarah to bed with it, the baby listening to the music as she drifted off to sleep.

Sarah's parents divorced when she was four, and Sarah's mother lost custody of her. Although she was very small, Sarah associated that music box with her mother. It became her most cherished possession, but she never allowed anyone else to wind up the music box and play it for her before she went to sleep. When Sarah was lonesome for her mom, she would wind up the music box, let it play, and cry herself to sleep. It wasn't until she was a teenager and reunited with her mother that she learned her mother bought an identical music box and played it when she was crying for Sarah.

CREATE FAMILY TRADITIONS

Family traditions may have changed during a divorce, but they need not be lost entirely. A divorced parent has the opportunity to create new traditions and new definitions of their new family—and the child can be involved in the process as well.

These traditions can be as simple as having hamburgers every Saturday night or taking a walk on Sunday afternoons, to more elaborate traditions for vacations and holidays.

Ask your children for ideas on how to make the holidays special, what special foods they like, and what special activities they want the family to participate in. One idea might be taking pictures and keeping them in a family album, which establishes a family history and shows the children that their past is important. Talk to your children about family history. Even if the traditions a family has no longer match up with those of the culture they come from, most children want to know what it means to be part of a particular religion or nationality; these are important parts of your children's background.

DISTINGUISH BETWEEN THE BEHAVIOR AND THE CHILD

Criticizing children's behavior, rather than the children themselves, teaches them acceptable behavior without damaging their self-esteem or threatening their place in the family. One way of doing this is to phrase criticism in terms of *your feelings* about the child's behavior, rather than passing down a judgment on the children themselves. "I feel angry when I don't have quiet time to read" is better than "You make me mad because you are so noisy all the time."

When you distinguish between the behavior and the child, tell what was done wrong and either explain or show how it can be done better. From this kind of criticism, your child understands that you believe he or she can improve and change and that you are involved enough to give direction.

ENCOURAGE A SENSE OF UNIQUENESS

Another element of children's self-esteem is their sense of who they personally are—their personal identity. In what ways are they special and different from everyone else? Are these differences positive or negative, acceptable or unacceptable? Parents are not the only ones who influence their children's self-esteem in this area, but they can help them a great deal in seeing how their personalities are both different and acceptable.

Children, especially young children, have no way of knowing how some things are different from others. They may ask questions or have thoughts unique to themselves that they assume everyone has, or they may discover something quite universal that they believe to be especially theirs. When children do discover something different about themselves, they may be apprehensive; they need help in evaluating each characteristic.

Whether a child's differences are positive—he has artistic talent; or negative—she hits other children more than anyone else in nursery school; the child needs to know that his or her personality characteristics and himself or herself are *related*, but not *identical*. Thus, "I notice you hit the other kids a lot. You must have some mad feelings, but it's not good to hit people" is better than "You're violent and destructive. You'll end up in jail someday!"

Similarly, "You can sure paint good trees and landscapes" shows children that they have talent, without setting up the label of "You're a good artist"—an expectation children may feel they have to live up to even if they lose interest in it.

As a parent, it is easy to be afraid that even if *you* accept your child's differences, society may not. We tend to teach our children to conform because we are worried that if they don't they won't get a job, they won't be liked, they won't get along with their teachers—it may be this more than any personal offense that makes parents say things like, "You look terrible, go change those clothes!" or "You can't go around talking like that!"

While children need to know the rules of their society, they also need room to experiment with thoughts and behavior that are outside the tried and true methods. Chances are the children who want to dye their hair purple at twelve will not want the same thing at twenty. Of course, parents have to draw the line at safety; some experiments may be damaging or fatal if they involve drugs, dangerous places and people, or criminal behavior.

Children's sense of their own specialness needs to be balanced with their desire to conform to the group. Some children may have a fear of seeming different in *any* way, while others may be afraid that if they're "just like everybody else," they will lose their parents' or teachers' love.

Sometimes children may have particularly creative ideas in dealing with problems in their own lives. Because they often may not know established methods of coping with problems, they may come up with solutions that are actually better! Parents can encourage this by *asking* them, "Do you have any ideas about how we could decorate your room . . . keep your hamsters in their cage . . . make your clothes easier to reach?" Encouraging your children to explore and have fun with their own ideas helps build a coping skill that will be invaluable when they grow up. Let your children know that there are no limits on their thoughts; that anything, no matter how off-the-wall, can be considered and that their ideas will not be ridiculed.

Children who are encouraged to value their own thoughts, to question and analyze and stick up for their own ideas, will not only have high self-esteem but are more likely to have high intelligence as well. As much as possible, let your children know that there are many ways to accomplish a task, and that they need not always follow your way of doing things—that there is not a right and wrong way of doing things.

Parents are an important part of children's self-esteem, but one of the most important things parents can do is know when to stay *out* of a child's life. Give your children privacy. Make sure they have some space to call their own. Encourage them to keep a diary, and *don't read it*.

Although it is important to let your kids know that it's OK to share their feelings with you, it is not necessarily true that in a "close" family children will want to tell their parents everything they feel. Children need to be able to think their own thoughts, hold their own conversations with friends, and do what they want to do—within reasonable and safe limits—in their free time. This is just basic courtesy and respect. Don't demand that they tell you what they're thinking or what their friends said. Children who know that their thoughts, feelings, and actions will be treated with respect are far more likely to be responsible with them, and they will usually give others the same respect.

Some positive affirmations for a child's sense of specialness are "I love you and there's no one in the world like you," "Everything about you is special," or "It's OK to be different from other people."

NURTURE YOUR CHILDREN

Parenting involves nurturing. It is a seven-day-a-week, twenty-four-hour-a-day job. However, there are times when we slip and don't always do what's best, but it isn't always harmful.

For example, most parents try to provide wholesome, nutritious food for themselves and their children. However, there are some days when it is easier to give in and let the kids eat junk food than to prepare the right foods for them. Joyce has always been a good mother to Jeanine and Joylene. She keeps her cupboards well stocked with good food as well as some junk food, and she makes them eat well-balanced meals six days a week. However, Saturday is everyone's day off. Joyce sleeps in and doesn't bother cooking at all on Saturday. Whatever the kids crave and can find or buy, they can eat. No attempt is made to chide them for wrong choices. If they want chocolate cake and chocolate ice cream for breakfast, candy bars and a package of cookies for lunch, and cupcakes, potato chips, and caramel corn for dinner, that is fine. They are even welcome to wash it all down with a gallon of soda! However, they had better be prepared to suffer the consequences and receive no sympathy from Mom.

Nutritionally, it probably all balances itself out because the children soon realize it may not be worth overindulging on junk foods if they are too sick to enjoy the day.

Psychological junk food, however, is a different story. As parents, and especially single parents, our psychological cupboards should be well stocked with psychologically sound mental and emotional food. However, when thrown off balance by a divorce and all the pressures that it involves, sometimes we don't have the strength to dish up a good helping of psychologically sound affirmations and praise to develop a child's self-esteem. Like the mom who let her kids eat whatever they wanted on Saturday, we sometimes fall into the habit of only giving our kids junk food psychologically, not only on Saturday, but every day when we come home from work and are physically and emotionally spent.

Unfortunately, that may be all we have in the cupboard, and if that's true, that is what we are going to feed the kids. Junk food in the form of insults, complaints, nagging, put-downs, yelling, anger, and attacks on the children's other parent does not help the child develop psychologically. We can only nourish from overflow, not emptiness. If we aren't kind and loving to ourselves, how can we be kind and loving to our children?

Some children are sufficiently strong in self-esteem and seemingly are not dependent upon strokes from their parents. If the parent has low self-esteem, this could be a real threat to the parent. Consciously or unconsciously they may embark on a crusade to bring the child down to their level. Rather than praise their child and recognize achievements, they may continually criticize and point out shortcomings. The audio cassette series *Parenting with Love and Logic*, by Fay, Cline, and Shaw,[1] describes how we should allow natural consequences to behaviors. According to Jim Fay, we gain control when we give *some* control to kids. Many children are crippled psychologically by their parents, who were likewise crippled psychologically by their parents. Our self-concept is not inherited genetically, but it is directly related to our parents' self-concept. Children identify with their parents and use that identity as an unconscious standard to measure themselves against.

The treatment parents give their children reflects their feelings for their own selves. Parents have a natural desire to have their children be like them and identify with their ideals, communicating it consciously and unconsciously.

Many of our actions cannot be given a logical explanation, other than we have seen our parents do the same thing so we do it without question.

Children who have gone through a divorce suffer from

a loss of self-esteem. The things children base their identity on—associations with parents, siblings, school, family traditions, even geographic locations—can all change at once, leaving the children no longer sure of who they are. Many emotions they may never have experienced before can make them feel out of control, alienated, and unacceptable.

In addition, during a divorce parents and children may have their emotional resources stretched to the breaking point. Parents may be less affectionate, less patient, less able to listen and spend time with their children, because their own emotions are in such chaos. Yet a child going through a divorce needs more of these things than ever before in order to have good self-esteem.

16

Few things help an individual more than to place responsibility upon him, and to let him know that you trust him.
Booker T. Washington

Teaching Children to Become Self-Sufficient

When a mother eagle decides it's time for her young ones to learn how to fly, she rearranges the twigs in their nest so they stick straight up rather than laying flat, making the nest uncomfortable. One by one she gently pushes the eaglets out of the nest in order to force them to learn to fly. Watching ever so carefully, she allows the eaglet to flutter and try out its wings until it becomes tired; then she swoops down underneath her faltering young one and catches it on her wings, carrying it back to the safety of the nest. She repeats this process over and over until each of her eaglets is able to fly without her assistance.

Divorce is not the time to push your young ones out of the nest, but the divorce process itself makes the nest uncomfortable and provides a good time to teach children of all ages to become more self-sufficient and responsible. More than likely, after the divorce the custodial parent has twice as many responsibilities and half as much emotional support. Many single parents compare their increased burdens and responsibilities to feeling like a rubber band stretched to the breaking point and ready to snap. The best way to remedy this situation is to explain the problem to the children and ask for their help in appropriate areas.

By giving your children additional responsibilities after the divorce (not just busywork), you not only help them feel like they are an intricate and important part of the family but expedite their growth and healing processes as well. Children, as well as adults, are more likely to live up to their responsibilities if they understand them. It is extremely important for you to clearly explain what is expected and to be consistent about it. If you tell your child, "From now on you're to take the garbage out," and forget about it the next week, your child learns that responsibility is never long-term. If a child neglects to do the work, it should remain undone, within reason. At the same time, parents must have some flexibility in special circumstances. Rules that are too rigid make children feel that the rules are more important than they are.

Chores are not just to help make the parents' lives easier; they also have the purpose of helping children feel good about themselves, feel productive, and feel they are a giving as well as a receiving part of the family. Some parents think it is cruel to make a child work at home. They say, "I never had to do chores as a child. . . . Let children be children." However, research has shown that children who are responsible and giving are more likely to become adults who are responsible and giving, and possibly become leaders as well.

Another added benefit of responsibilities is that they provide routine, structure, limitations, and a feeling of security—all of which are important for children while going through the divorce and healing process. As positive as all these benefits are, there's one problem with responsibility: children don't like to accept it. So parents need to develop a system that will encourage children to do so. One method of doing this is employing a responsibility chart.

Make a list of all the household responsibilities, including going to work and bringing home a paycheck; banking; planning meals; buying groceries; carrying in the groceries from the car; putting them away; doing the laundry; taking children to the doctor, dentist, and school activities; and maintaining and repairing the car and house. Also include chores like mowing the lawn, washing the dishes, cleaning the bathrooms, making the beds, taking out the trash, setting the table, clearing the table, loading the dishwasher or washing the dishes, sorting the laundry, putting a load of wash in the washing machine, hanging them on the line or transferring them to the dryer, folding the clothes, etc. Now go over your list and identify which ones must be done by you and which ones you can appropriately delegate to your children. Then call a family meeting and say something like this:

"Kids, we are a whole and complete family. We are a real team. And all teams have positions. For example, on a baseball team there is a first-base player, a second-base player, a third-base player, a pitcher, a catcher, a shortstop, and outfielders. All of the players on the team are very important for that team to work. If one member of the team, such as the first baseman, decides not to work or be a part of the team, the baseball team won't win many games. You are also very important members of this team, and you each have a special part in making us a family. So it is important that we all have our own responsibilities, just like the first baseman who has to be ready to catch the ball.

"I have a list of all the responsibilities in our home that make our team work, or make our home work. As I read the list, think about the things that you like to do. As I go through this list, if you would rather not do an item, you don't have to volunteer for that responsibility. However, after I have read all the responsibilities on the list, I, as umpire, will decide who will take the leftover items on the list. So let's get started . . ."

Begin by reading the first chore on the list. If no one takes this responsibility, don't say anything, just move on to the next one. When you get to the end of the list, look at the responsibilities that have not been taken, and then assign them to each of your children.

Once this is done, provide each child with a blank chart or make whatever works best for your family situation. Many stationery stores or teacher supply houses have ready-made charts that are ideal for this purpose. Tell your children to write their names at the top and list all of the chores they have chosen for the coming week or month, then fill in the days of the week in the appropriate boxes. After this, make a small *x* next to each of the days the children are responsible for that activity. For example, you may take the trash out on Monday, Wednesday, and Friday, so you would put a small *x* in the boxes representing Monday, Wednesday, and Friday. Since beds need to be made every day, all the boxes get an *x* every day. Some chores will be done once a week, so tell them to put an *x* next to the day they intend to do that chore. A bonus list might include chores such as mowing the lawn in the summertime and shoveling snow off the sidewalk in the winter.

Create your own guidelines about the chores. Some families change chores every month, while others change every week. Many families also allow the kids to trade chores during the week if they have a conflict. Decide what works best in your situation.

The next thing to do is to explain the rules about how you expect the chores to be done and what happens when they aren't done. Some kids prefer to do their chores after school. The early risers might prefer to do their chores in the morning. However, each evening the children should check the chart to make sure they completed all chores assigned for that day. If they are all completed, draw a circle around those items or put a star or sticker in the appropriate box. If not completed, the chores are to be done as soon as their homework is finished and before they go to bed. If it is already too late, the child should get up earlier the next morning and complete the chore before going to school. If this happens, the children will *not* receive a circle or star around their *x*. They also won't get credit because the chore wasn't done in the assigned time, but they will still have to complete the responsibility. At the end of the week the children will total their points. Parents should decide in advance the total amount of points the children should be allowed for performing each chore, for example 5-15 points per chore completed.

Some people object to paying children for performing their responsibilities, and this is a valid point. However, it would be difficult for an adult to rationalize working without pay for a week. You also want to consider that the child needs a way to earn some money of his own and this is a good way to do it. Teaching a child about money by paying him or her for performing chores gives the child a better sense of the value of money than just handing it out whenever the child requests it or always saying, "I don't have enough money to give any to you." Decide upon your own reward system, depending upon your financial situation and your values.

I believe children should be rewarded for what they have done. So I suggest that you take a total number, that they have done that week (say, 5 chores a day times 7 days), and multiply it by the number of cents that would fit your budget. For example, if each chore is worth five points or cents and they performed all thirty-five chores, they would receive $1.75 per week. Each child should feel that he or she is as important as the others. However, if a five-year-old is receiving the same amount as a seventeen-year-old, you are likely to have a revolt on your hands. You must consider the child's age, the extent of the responsibilities, the child's financial needs, and the value of the services performed. If the value is assigned to the chore rather than the child, some of the younger children might want to take on a responsibility normally reserved for an older child. It might be a good idea to assign point values, instead of monetary values, that can be accumulated and "cashed in" toward an individual or family treat. You are the umpire, so you decide what is fair.

Keeping the household running properly and helping with chores is only one aspect of teaching responsibility. Other areas are just as crucial.

MAKE SURE YOUR CHILDREN LEARN BASIC SURVIVAL SKILLS

Children need to learn to assume responsibility for their basic needs. Don't worry about starting too young. Even two-year-olds have preferences about their clothing. That doesn't mean you always let them choose, but you can keep matching shirts and pants together in their closet or drawer so that they get to accept the responsibility of deciding what to wear (within weather and occasion parameters). Most four-year-olds can empty the wastebasket, take the flatware out of the dishwasher, put their own clothes in the hamper, and many other chores.

Jayme was only three when her mother taught her how to clean the bathroom sinks. Even though she couldn't reach the sink from her stool, her mother sat her on the countertop, gave her a wet sponge and some cleansing powder, and let her work on it until it was clean. Although the sink never was cleaned to perfection and there were plenty of traces of the cleansing powder left over, Jayme learned that keeping the sinks clean was her responsibility, and she cheerfully and willingly did them every week. As she grew older, she accepted more and more of the household responsibilities and became more proficient at them.

Jayme's sister, Somer, was six when she started fixing breakfast for both of them. Although it started with cold cereal, fruit, and juice, she soon learned to heat and serve prepared foods in the microwave. By the time Somer was eight she could fix eggs and toast or french toast for their breakfast. That became one of her favorite household responsibilities. Each morning Somer is responsible for fixing breakfast for herself and Jayme while Mom gets ready for work.

Begin early to teach your children the basics of fixing something to eat, planning meals, buying ingredients for those meals, and looking for the best prices. Also, as much as possible, allow children to choose how their room is to be arranged and decorated. Teach them to be responsible for the cleanliness and good repair of their own clothing.

Although the basics of clothing care may seem natural to some adults, to children it can be one of the unsolved mysteries of the world. George was eleven when he realized he didn't have any clean socks to wear to school one day. Confident he could handle the situation without his mother, he found the "perfect solution" . . . the electric mixer could serve as a mini-washing machine! Filling the mixing bowl with hot water and detergent, he turned it on, let the lather rise, and dropped in his socks. Quickly he learned the difference between a washing machine agitator and the beaters on an electric mixer. Probably no one noticed that George wore dirty socks to school that day (except those who came too close), but when his mother arrived home she did notice something resembling a wet muskrat in the mixing bowl. That night George received his first lesson on doing laundry.

Take advantage of every teachable moment. When you are doing the laundry or mending clothes, show the kids what you are doing and why, so they will be able to do it themselves when necessary. Divorced kids frequently live in one-parent homes, and that parent may leave for work before the kids leave for school. Some days kids need to wear specific items of clothing for gym class, chorus, or extra-curricular activities. If Mom has already left for work and kids pop a button, tear the hem out, or realize the clothes are dirty, they need to be able to take care of it themselves. Being self-sufficient in this area doesn't mean they have to take care of all their clothing maintenance, but it will give them more control over various situations in which they may find themselves, and occasionally prevent being embarrassed by torn or dirty clothing. Show your children how to sort the laundry and wash their clothes as soon as they can reach the controls on the machines. Teach young boys and girls how to sew on a button, repair a zipper, hem their clothes by ironing on hemming tape or using masking tape. If possible, enroll your girls *and* boys in a children's sewing class.

Erynn was only seven when she started taking a children's sewing class and making some clothes for herself. When Emily, her nine-year-old sister, saw what a great job Erynn did and how much pleasure she received from making her own clothes, she decided she wanted to take a sewing class too. After a year and a half of lessons one day a week, at a cost of $5 per hour, they have each made blouses, skirts, dresses, and pants for themselves and are now making gifts for their cousins. They are more proud of these clothes than the most expensive clothes that hang in their closet, and rightfully so. As adults, they may choose not to make their own clothes, but as children they have been given the wonderful confidence-building experience of selecting their own fabric, choosing a pattern they like, making their own clothes, and feeling that they know how to assume responsibility for another area of their lives.

TEACH THEM HOW TO MAKE RESPONSIBLE CHOICES

Children need to understand that they are responsible for their choices. It is easy to protect children from the consequences of their behavior, but this will only confuse them. If they can make their decisions based on having something to lose and something to gain, it will be easier for them to realize the natural consequences of their decisions. At the same time, there must be margin for error. If your kids spend all of their lunch money on a toy rather than on lunch, don't make them go without lunch for a week. However, make sure the value of that toy is deducted from the amount of money they would have received for their allowance. You must teach your children to take responsibility for their mistakes without making them suffer physically or psychologically for them. Children who come home after curfew, for example, might be grounded for a few days, but they should not find themselves locked out of the house (it's illegal)! They will learn to be responsible for their mistakes and successes when they realize that Mom or Dad is not always going to bail them out of their problems. This is a form of discipline, not punishment.

SHOW THEM HOW TO SET GOALS

Teaching children how to set and achieve goals helps them take one giant step forward in learning to be responsible. Understanding how goals are set and achieved gives a child a sense of order and purpose. These can be daily, weekly, or monthly goals. Here's what you need to do.

Sit down with your children, and ask them to write down some goals for themselves. Don't set goals for them! Let them decide what they want to accomplish and whether they want to share their goals with you or other members of the family. The first goals should be basic and easy to accomplish—a clean room, learning a skill, reading a certain number of books. By keeping the goals simple and short-term, children will experience a feeling of achievement and satisfaction. They will learn that no one else reaches these goals for them; they alone are responsible for setting and achieving them. Make sure they understand that their goals should include things they have control over—their own behavior and actions, not the behavior and actions of other people. For example, help them realize they can't reach a goal of ''getting Mommy and Daddy back together.''

DEVELOP THEIR VALUE SYSTEM

Share your values with your children, and teach them moral principles to govern their behavior. Don't just give them rules, but explain the principles and values behind them. Discussing fairness, responsibility, and integrity will help a child understand how to evaluate his or her own behavior. You might also want to take your children to the local library and check out the Value Tale Books by Dr. Spencer Johnson.[1] Each beautifully illustrated book tells about one famous person and how his or her actions exemplified certain values. Read them together as a family activity. Discuss each person and his experiences and how that same value applies to your children's activities. After you read this series, try reading biographies of famous people and asking your children to identify the values these people portrayed.

Although very young children are not capable of understanding the subtle points of ethics, they can understand concepts like fairness. An excellent series of books to teach values to young children are those written by Joy Berry,[2] which are probably available at your school library or local bookstore.

Although it is helpful to talk about your values, it is even better for the child to see them in action. A seventeen-year-old boy said, "My mother and father never sat me down and told me what values and morals to have. But by watching them and seeing what was important to them, I was able to form good, strong beliefs that I chose for myself. This makes me want to abide by them even more than if I had just been told what to do."

A child's value system may be different from his or her parents'. In a divorced family, the child often has two sets of values to deal with, Mom's and Dad's. The child's own may be a combination of the two, or it may contain paradoxes. If a parent allows a child to question and discuss values rather than just laying down the law, the child has a chance to challenge and question his or her own beliefs as well as the parents', so the child's value system will truly become his or her own. No matter how concerned they are, parents cannot arbitrarily decide their children's values. Parents model their own values and can set rules that exemplify these values, but ultimately the choice is with the child.

Whatever their values, children need to realize how much better they feel about themselves when they abide by their values (whether set by themselves or their parents initially) than when their behavior is a violation of their values or those values their parents asked them to abide by. Even a rebellious teenager most often will return to many of his parents' values in his twenties.

BUILD DECISION-MAKING SKILLS

Decision making is a process that is learned. So you will need to discuss with your children how to make decisions. The first step is teaching them that decisions are based on understanding the potential outcomes and consequences.

The "Benjamin Franklin Decision Method" is a good place to start. Take a piece of notebook paper and draw a line across the first line of the paper. Then divide the sheet down the middle with another line. At the top of the page, create a heading area and write down the decision that needs to be made. Label the left-hand column "For" and the right-hand column "Against." Then list all the reasons in favor of the decision in the left-hand column, and list all the reasons against the decision in the right-hand column. See if the number of items in favor of the decision outweighs the number against the decision.

You'll also need to show children how their value system determines the decisions they make. For example, what do they value most: having money in their bank account for fun activities like a camping trip or sporting event, or spending their money and borrowing on next month's allowance in order to get the model airplane they just can't live without right now?

When children understand the importance of values in decision making, they will base their decisions on their values rather than on what is easy. Work with your children on some of the decisions they need to make. Use it as an opportunity to give them examples of how their values determine the choices and decisions they make.

MODEL GOOD PROBLEM-SOLVING TECHNIQUES

During the aftermath of divorce, both parents generally acquire new skills that they had previously depended upon the other parent to perform. If you saw the movie *Kramer vs. Kramer*, you probably remember the funny scenes in which the young child was watching his father learn how to cook. Don't hesitate to allow your children to see your imperfections or inadequacies. A dad who makes a mess in the kitchen trying to learn how to cook models different problem-solving techniques than a dad who doesn't try to cook and only feeds his kids food from a fast-food restaurant. Likewise, a mom who buys a tool kit of her own and tries to figure out how to repair the garage door opener or take apart, clean, and repair the lawn mower is setting a good example for her children. If money was available, someone would be hired to perform the task. But since money is a problem, rather than leaving the task undone, the parent tries to figure out a way to solve the problem. Children learn to apply these trial-and-error skills to their own problems.

Show your children how problems can be broken down into parts, identified, and solved. Teach them to look at the problem from many different angles, using brainstorming as a technique. Consider any solution that comes to mind, no matter how ridiculous it may appear at first. Remind them that solutions often come in pieces and interact just like the pieces of a puzzle.

When children learn how to analyze a problem, find information resources, study the information, consider various solutions, and attempt to resolve the problem by trial and error, they become confident about their own problem-solving skills. This confidence results in accepting and fulfilling their responsibilities rather than giving up or remaining totally dependent upon Mom or Dad.

After his parents' divorce, nine-year-old Mark began to astutely observe each parent in their separate households as he tried to sort out who was to blame for the divorce. In the process he noticed a basic difference in the way they handled problems. Dad frequently gave up and considered a situation hopeless when the odds seemed overwhelmingly against him. Mom seemed to do best when the situation looked hopeless and would often resort to some unorthodox methods of solving the problem, which frequently embarrassed Mark even though they worked. One day right after Mark and his mom moved to a new neighborhood, he ran hurriedly out the door to ride his bike to school so he wouldn't be late for an important test. Much to his dismay, the tire was flat. He didn't have a tire pump and the closest gas station was five miles away. Dad lived out of state and Mom was still on her way to work. If he walked to school he would miss his test. In his frustration, he got angry and kicked the bike tire. Then he thought, "What would Dad do?" He answered that question with, "He would stay home and wait until he could get someone to fix the tire for him." Then he thought, "What would Mom do?" He answered that question with, "She would find someone to help her."

Even though in the past Mark had frequently been embarrassed by his mother's asking strangers for assistance when they needed help (after all, real men don't ask for directions or assistance), he realized it was a way to resolve problems. Mustering up all the courage he could and putting aside his embarrassment, Mark knocked on the doors of several neighbors until he found one with a tire pump. Not only were they more than willing to loan him the pump, but they commended him for being such a responsible young boy and finding a solution to his problems so he wouldn't miss an important test at school.

Solving his problem this way was a major breakthrough for Mark. Once he realized that asking others for help was a solution that worked, he gained confidence in his ability to solve problems and assumed even more responsibilities.

TEACH YOUR CHILDREN THAT THEY ARE RESPONSIBLE FOR THEIR EMOTIONS

A necessary ingredient of responsibility is accepting the consequences of one's emotional reactions. Children need to understand that they have a choice about how to react. They can choose to behave responsibly when they feel happy, sad, or angry, and they should not blame others for their reactions. "He made me so mad I had to hit him" is not a responsible emotional reaction. Help your children set their own limits on acceptable or unacceptable ways of dealing with their emotions. Regardless of how angry, happy, or sad they might be, they must be taught they can't knock over lamps or throw tantrums. Show them acceptable ways of venting this anger— whether it is screaming into their pillows, hitting a punching bag, or playing basketball, tennis, or some other active sport.

Children generally find ways to deal with their emotions by finding out how much they can get away with and by watching how their parents and other role models deal with their emotions.

During the difficult days after the children find out about the divorce and until they learn to accept it, they need help in realizing that they can choose their response to their feelings and that they are responsible for the consequences of their behavior.

If you give your children responsibility with respect and sensitivity, they will accept it. Like the mother eagle, however, you need to be ready to swoop down and rescue them if they begin to falter. Children who learn to accept responsibility at a young age generally have an easier time as adults than children who have had everything done for them by their parents or others.

17

Enlisting the Support of Others

To me, divorce means shattered love, shattered hope, shattered trust, shattered dreams . . . my whole life is shattered.

Fifteen-year-old girl

When your marriage broke up, it may have felt as if your world and your children's lives had crumbled and fallen apart. Divorce gives new meaning to the Humpty Dumpty nursery rhyme we all learned as children:

> Humpty Dumpty sat on a wall,
> Humpty Dumpty had a great fall;
> All the King's horses and all the King's men
> Couldn't put Humpty together again.

Right now you might feel like Humpty Dumpty . . . broken and beyond being fixed. Even if all the pieces were intact, and the King's horses and the King's men used the best glue in the world, there would be plenty of cracks to betray that something traumatic had happened.

Most children's books picture Humpty Dumpty as an egg; and we can easily understand how difficult it would be to put an egg back together although we need to realize that families are not as fragile as eggs. They are far more resilient. True, divorce shatters our lifestyle and our family, but only temporarily. We can, however, use it as an opportunity to get closer to one another, find out our strengths and weaknesses, redefine our purposes and goals, regroup, and develop new patterns of living. Divorce allows us to establish new parameters and grow into an entirely new person with the help of those who function as King's horses and King's men in our lives.

Who are these royal helpers? Whomever you call on for assistance in time of need. More than likely it will be your extended family, friends, coworkers, your child's schoolteachers, school secretaries, and other people prominent in your lives such as scout leaders, athletic coaches, counselors, Sunday school teachers, ministers . . . the selection is unlimited.

After a divorce, the children's aunts, uncles, and grandparents make excellent companions for them because of their familiarity with the situation, the children, and their ability to understand what the kids are going through. Divorce also gives the family members a chance to spend quality time with the children. Remember that it is not how often one visits, but what transpires during that visit.

When asked, "Who helped you the most during the divorce and how?" a nine-year-old boy said, "My grandfather, because he was the substitute for my dad." One six-year-old girl said, "My mom and her two sisters." A twelve-year-old boy responded, "My mom and grandma were always there for me."

Children have many questions about divorce. Most frequently they ask, "If Dad can leave me, will Mom leave me too?" One five-year-old girl remarked, "My mom helped me the most by telling me she would always be with me." Another prominent question is, "If my mommy and daddy are divorced, do I still have a grandmother, aunt, or cousin?" Extended family members can answer these questions and set a child's mind at ease by assuring him or her that they still love them and will always be a part of their families.

One essential element in assuring the children's ability to cope with divorce is stability. In their world, where everything is changing all around them, things that are familiar can be comforting and reassuring. Grandparents, especially, should try to maintain familiar family traditions such as dinners, vacations, or gift giving.

Depending upon their reaction to the divorce, those on the outside can be a comforting means of support and security to you and your children and may give you not only the helping hand you need, but provide a source of stability in your rapidly changing world. There is one catch, however, in that you are responsible for informing them of the problem and asking for their help.

How many times have you heard doctors and various medical commercial messages inform you that "You are responsible for your own health"? Doctors can assist you if you find a problem, but you are responsible for being on the lookout for symptoms or any abnormalities in your body's physical condition. The American Cancer Society provides you with a list of danger signs. The American Heart Association tells you what you should be eating and how you should be exercising if you want to avoid heart trouble. If you sense a problem, you have it checked out.

Divorce is just like that. Everyone has problems . . . adults and children. Some have more serious problems than others, and for some the problems last longer. We want to help you identify potential problems, find sources of help, and minimize or eliminate the problems as soon as possible.

You, as well as your children and ex-spouse, need the love and support of family and friends during and after the divorce. No family should isolate itself. Others can help expedite the healing process. Divorce is difficult and painful, but trying to go through it without the help of others only drags out the pain. Ask for assistance from your friends when you are going through a divorce. Offer your assistance to friends who are going through a divorce, even if the pain is sometimes unbearable for you.

Poor, fragile Humpty Dumpty was broken and could not be put back together again. Unlike Humpty Dumpty, the broken and shattered pieces of your life *can* be put back together again. Your inner strength provides the superglue you need. The King's horses and the King's men come in the form of help from your extended family and friends. Don't be afraid to ask them for help. You will be whole again, even though the shape of your family unit and your life will be different. Many times, different can be better.

YOUR PARENTS' REACTION

We would all like to believe that Mom and Dad will be there for us regardless of how the rest of the world treats us. In most cases this is true. Mom's time-tested advice and Dad's wisdom, combined with their unconditional love, is an unbeatable combination when life has knocked us down. They know us well enough that they can overlook our moments of temporary insanity without judging us.

Unfortunately, when it comes to divorce, not all adults can rely on their own parents' acceptance of the decision. Our family's reactions can be as diverse as their reasons for such reactions.

Many parents are horrified over a divorce. If they did not realize there were serious problems in the relationship, they may react with shock and dismay. Also they may be resentful because they were not taken into their child's confidence. It is not uncommon for a parent to feel that it was their own fault for not having raised their child properly or helping prepare him or her for the responsibilities of married life. If parents don't believe in divorce, they will not be prone to accept what their daughter or son is doing and may reject or disown their own child.

Dave and Nikki were happily married for twelve years and had four children. Dave's parents owned the business in which he had worked since high school and which would some day belong to Dave. Nikki was a part of the family and dearly loved by her in-laws. When Dave became involved with his secretary and told Nikki he had filed for divorce, his parents immediately took Nikki's side. Being very opposed to divorce on religious grounds, they told Dave that if he left Nikki and the children, he would no longer have a job with them and would not inherit the business.

Dave left Nikki, his children, and the family business anyway. Nikki and the children spend all the holidays with Dave's family. And his parents have made it very plain to Dave that he can come visit them but is not to bring his new wife. Losing one's children, parental support, and livelihood doesn't help start a new marriage on solid ground. At last report, Dave's four-year-old marriage to his new wife was floundering. He still makes regular contact with his parents, however, and has not given up his hope that someday they will accept him regardless of his marital partner.

If your parents find it necessary to lecture or say, "I told you so," they are not giving you the support you need. Most people going through a divorce are mature adults who have reached their decision after careful thought and introspection. While it is easy for your parents to fall back into the habit of treating you like a child, especially if you are no longer married and have returned home to live with them, scolding or playing "If only . . ." is inappropriate and only serves their own purposes. By the same token, coddling or spoiling will only serve to slow the healing process, discourage growth, and hinder the rediscovery of your independence and autonomy.

Some parents find it difficult to see their child experiencing a lot of pain, or they are in so much emotional pain themselves that they cannot handle their child's divorce. Many parents see the divorce as a reflection of their own failure as a parent. Other parents are so embarrassed and humiliated that a divorce is happening in their family (especially if their religion actively opposes divorce) that they try to hide it from their friends and deny that it is happening. It may be so difficult for them that they find it necessary to keep their distance from their own kids. This, of course, only magnifies the pain for their children because their loss has now been doubled.

How about you? Are you disappointed with your parents' reaction to your divorce? Have they turned against you, or have they come to your defense and turned against your "no-good ex-spouse" with a vengeance? What is a proper response on their part? What is the healthiest for you and your children?

Here are some guidelines for relationships with your parents during and after divorce.

1. Tell them about the divorce before someone else does.

2. Try to be as objective as possible about the reason for the divorce.

3. Ask them to remain neutral regardless of how much venom is spit out regarding your ex-spouse. Tell them you need an objective sounding board for your feelings, and you may later resent any negative comments they make about your ex, even when made with the best of intentions. ("We never did think that bum was good enough for you.") After all, you did love this person at one time and he or she is the biological parent of your children.

4. Ask them not to alienate your ex-spouse. You want them to leave their relationship intact for the sake of the children.

5. Ask your parents not to say anything negative about your ex-spouse in front of your children.

6. Tell them when you don't feel like talking about the divorce.

7. Tell them if you want to talk about the divorce. You bring it up . . . don't wait for them to do so.

8. Tell them that you and the children have special

needs right now, one of which is to be alone occasionally, so please do not be offended during those times.

9. Tell them you and the children may need to be with them more than before, and ask them to include you in their lives as much as possible without interfering or causing them to resent their lack of privacy.

10. Ask them to give extra love and attention to your children during this transition time.

If your parents refuse to treat you like an adult and refuse to accept or respect your decision about the divorce, make your visits with them dependent upon not discussing it. Leave the door open emotionally so this difference of opinion does not destroy your relationship. Do not attempt to argue the point.

YOUR EX-IN-LAWS

"I love you as long as you make my son or daughter happy . . ." is an unspoken but all too familiar theme regarding relationships with former in-laws.

Unfortunately, it may be very difficult for you or your ex-spouse to maintain a good relationship with each other's parents. Natural resentments and the tendency for parents to take their own children's side in disputes lend themselves to strained relations between ex-spouses and their in-laws.

Suzanne was extremely close to her father-in-law, Wayne, during her twenty-year marriage to his son, Robert. From the very beginning Suzanne and Wayne had a loving and fun relationship. Wayne often told Suzanne he felt closer to her than to his son. Likewise, Suzanne had a better relationship with her father-in-law than with her own father. When Suzanne and Robert divorced, Wayne severed all relations with Suzanne and let her know she was not welcome in his home any longer. Suzanne was stunned, and she grieved over the death of their twenty-year, father-daughter relationship. It was more painful for her than the termination of her marriage.

Although it was Robert who had divorced Suzanne, he convinced his parents it was all her fault. For ten years they remained hardened to her, but on each birthday and holiday Suzanne had the kids call their grandparents and write them a note. Finally, they ''forgave Suzanne'' and spoke to her for the first time at their granddaughter's wedding. Although the relationship will never be close again, at least they are now cordial.

Is this a frequent occurrence among former in-laws? Sadly, for many it is. When asked what other people could have done to help him survive the divorce, one nine-year-old boy wrote: ''Well, my dad could have called or wrote and so could his parents.'' While waiting for the wounds to heal, it is important for all concerned to try to maintain friendly relationships.

18

The Extended Family

When everybody is fighting over who gets me and for how long, I call my aunt and ask her if I can come over and spend the night. We play games together. It helps me forget all the bad stuff that is happening.

Eleven-year-old boy

Family members, if they remember to remain neutral, can be effective go-betweens for estranged couples. Acting as mediators, they can ease the burden of separation for the children and help maintain at least the appearance of cooperation and mutual respect between Mom and Dad.

The extended family can fill a special need for children from divorced homes and are a crucial part of divorce recovery and the growth process throughout their whole lives. They can serve as important role models for children in addition to performing helpful functions for the divorced parents.

During and after a divorce, relatives outside the immediate family become considerably more important to a child than ever before. Since his or her nuclear family has been redefined, he or she needs the identity and security of belonging to a larger family.

THE GRANDPARENTS' ROLE

Grandparents frequently suffer as much as the non-custodial parents because they have little or no contact with their grandchildren—particularly if they do not live in the same area. When the family unit was intact, the children may have spent vacations with them, but after the divorce, visitation requirements place the priority on the non-custodial parent.

For years, much emotional carnage was left in the wake of a system that was accustomed to promoting only the interests of the feuding parents. Now, however, nearly every state has laws guaranteeing the visitation rights of grandparents. And pending legislation may serve to promote those rights even further. Clearly, it is in the best interests of all parties to allow continuing contact between grandparents and grandchildren, keeping the fabric of the family as intact as possible.

Encourage your children to maintain contact with your ex-spouse's parents. Even if your ex's parents aren't particularly fond of you, your children should be kept out of any conflict. Allow them to send birthday cards and holiday greetings to both sets of grandparents.

Grandparents also need to be reminded not to take sides against the parents or speak unkindly about them in front of the children. If their son or daughter causes them to feel animosity toward their former son- or daughter-in-law, it may be hard for them to forgive and forget. Usually the spouses involved get over the bitterness eventually because they have expressed their anger in so many ways. This may not happen for the other relatives.

Those grandparents who have money will often have an easier time with visitation rights. In many cases the grandparents offer to pay part of the child support, or an additional amount of child support, so they can retain regular visitation rights.

Margaret and Ted were financially comfortable but their son, who was going through a divorce, only had a meager salary. The court ordered him to pay three hundred dollars a month in child support, but the grandparents offered to double it in exchange for regular visits with their grandchild. To them it was a small price to pay for someone who gave them so much happiness.

Dorothy was a wealthy grandmother with nine grandchildren, all of whom had divorced parents living in different states. Each year she arranged with her former daughters-in-law to have the grandchildren come visit her for one week in the summer. Dorothy also always bought their school clothes for them. It was fun for Dorothy and the children.

Money doesn't always make visitation possible, but it can makes visits easier to arrange. Those grandparents without a lot of money can find inexpensive ways to stay in contact with the children, much like the absent parent.

My children, Cheri and Brad, always knew my mother loved them. Since I worked many late hours for several years, my mother would call them and chat and tell them she was always there for them. They knew she wouldn't judge them if they didn't bring home all A's. When she baby-sat with Brad, the two would tell jokes to each other and play games.

Nelie and George provide a wonderful example of how meaningful grandparents can be in the lives of their grandchildren. Regardless of how much conflict there was between the parents, they always provided a haven for the grandchildren where neither parent would be criticized. They consistently offered unconditional love, support, and someone to talk to. Although they didn't have a lot of money, they occasional found a way to send the kids a twenty-dollar bill and an encouraging note.

Through the turbulent years of the divorce, Nelie and George offered a home away from both homes where there would be no emotional trauma. Everyone would meet at their home for "holidays," whether or not it was close to the holiday they were celebrating. As the grandkids grew up and went to college, they chose to spend their vacations at their grandparents' house and would call their parents and say, "Could you come visit me at Grandma's? I will be there during my vacation."

Both sets of parents were always welcome at Grandma's and Grandpa's, and everyone could visit without staking their territory or making the other parent feel excluded.

The bottom line in broken relationships is to be patient and continue to leave the door open for contact. Realize the importance of keeping extended family relationships intact. Allow the children to see both sets of grandparents, even if the grandparents aren't friendly toward you. Attempting to deny grandparents visitation simply incurs the wrath of yet another party, adding to the distress of everyone. Regardless of why the marriage ended, there is no such thing as ex-grandparents.

AUNTS, UNCLES, AND COUSINS

Six-year-old Natalie had a special love for Tami and Traci, her older cousins on her father's side. From birth they had made a special ceremony of presenting their outgrown clothes to Natalie and watching her try them on and anticipate growing into them. After the divorce separated them geographically, they continued to share their outgrown clothes with her. About twice a year they shipped Natalie their outgrown coats, school and church clothes, and sometimes even their bikes. Natalie preferred their clothes to new ones her mother bought her in the store. She would try to guess who bought the clothes for them, her father's mother or her Aunt Jeri, and talk about whether or not she thought they liked them and where they wore them. It was a small but significant way they continued to share their lives.

After Nathan's parents divorced, his visits with his relatives took on new meaning. He could always count on his Uncle Jim to take him on a motorcycle ride or play ball with him . . . activities Mom didn't excel in. Uncle Elwyn sometimes took him along on his delivery route, which resulted in a day full of fun and laughter.

Nathan's aunts kept up a special relationship with him

even though they lived many miles away. He could always count on receiving special packages in the mail from Aunt Jeri; not expensive gifts, but unique, fun things kids like that showed him she was thinking about him. Although she only got to see him two or three times a year, when they were together Aunt Cindy always took time to go for a walk with him and listen. Nathan spent many enjoyable hours with his Aunt Leni, playing games of his choice or being amused by tales of funny happenings in the family.

When Nathan went to college, his Uncle George lived five hours away, but he was always there when Nathan needed him, using his truck to move Nathan into and out of the dorm every year and to pick him up for school breaks. Whenever Nathan dated someone special, he made sure his uncles and aunts met her. Their approval was very important to him.

As Nathan grew older, he sought out and became acquainted with relatives on both sides of his family that he had never known or spent any time with—second cousins, great aunts and uncles, and others. He developed a special love for them, their spouses, and their children. He began to spend valuable time with them. Becoming acquainted with his mom's and dad's aunts, uncles, and cousins helped give him a sense of continuity and family that the divorce had taken away.

If family members ask, "Can I do anything to help?" tell them yes. Even if they don't ask, *tell* them your concerns about the situation and *ask* them to do the following for your children:

- Don't take sides; remain neutral.
- *Never* make derogatory remarks about the other parent in front of the children.
- Occasionally deliver the children to the non-custodial parent and pick them up again, or allow their home to be used as a pickup and delivery point to avoid confrontations.

- Be available to the kids if they want to talk, but don't try to pressure them to talk about the divorce or what is going on.
- Reassure the kids that their extended family members on both sides love them and are there for them.
- Invite the children to their home rather than visiting them in your home during the divorce. Kids need to spend time in a stable environment when theirs is falling apart.
- Include your kids in some of their family outings or activities.
- Keep in touch with the kids if you don't live close by. Send love notes. Make phone calls. Assure them of your continued interest and concern.
- Contact each child on his or her birthday. A present isn't necessary, but do remember it with a card or phone call.
- Remember the needs of each child to feel special. Be aware of sibling rivalry. Give each child as much individual attention as possible.

The attention and love of family members can be effective in assuring the happiness and well-being of children in a divorced family. By maintaining a loving and understanding relationship with all parties concerned, they can help create a harmonious and nurturing atmosphere in which all can grow.

19

Friends to the End?

When all Mommy felt like doing was staying home and crying, sometimes one of her friends would come pick me up and take me to a movie or shopping. It was lots of fun.

Eight-year-old girl

Friends as well as family will react to the news of your divorce in a variety of ways. Some people will rally to your assistance, and others will distance themselves from you. You also will find that your reactions to your friends may change.

Sometimes friends want to help so badly that their attention feels like an invasion of privacy. While your emotions are raw, it might be difficult to talk to others because the pain is too great. This refusal to talk might be viewed by your friends as an insult. Others, who were once considered close confidants, may feel alienated if they didn't know of the pending divorce in advance.

Married friends often discover that they feel awkward with a newly divorced friend. What can they talk about? How will they go out together without a fourth person? Jealousy also moves into the scene. Many women, including your friends, feel threatened by a newly divorced woman. And your men friends may look at you as a lonely woman in need of companionship. These feelings put many friends in an uncomfortable position . . . sometimes it's so uncomfortable that the friendship ends. And things aren't much better for newly divorced men. Married women are threatened by you too, because they are afraid that their husbands will see the single life as being better than married life. And perhaps they have also been having some marital problems and may worry that your divorce is catching.

And divorce does often shake the very foundation of your friends' marriages. "If John and Mary seemed so happily married all those years and they are getting divorced, I wonder if we are next?" or "Mary told me about a few problems, but I never dreamed it was this serious . . . could our problems lead to divorce too?" Others wonder, "If it happened to them, could it happen to us?"

Clearly, divorce is also a scary and difficult time for friends. If married friends were close to both the husband and wife, who will they keep as a friend after the divorce? Why can't they still be friends with both? Theoretically, everyone should remain friends, but in reality it doesn't always happen that way. Some couples will choose to remain with the woman because she was the one who worked to keep the friendship going when she was married, and they feel closer to her.

Divorced couples whose friends are from their church relationships or religious affiliations often find that their friends will rally to the support of the "victim" and will completely ostracize the person who left. This can be a real shock to the partner who is perceived as the culprit. Most often, this happens when another man or woman was involved in the breaking up of the relationship.

Sometimes people going through a divorce drop their old friends because the friends represent their life with their ex-spouse—a life to which they can never return. They may also find that they have nothing in common with the married friends anymore, so they seek friendships elsewhere. Be careful about dropping friends from your life, though. You might be throwing away precious jewels. It is better to put the friendship on hold for awhile or try to establish it on a different basis than to abandon it.

Because friends are one of a couples' most precious possessions, they are thrown into the battle along with the children, the house, and other assets. Oftentimes one of the spouses will move to a different social setting, but they still see old friends on many occasions, especially for the children's school events, Little League games, track meets, concerts, graduations, and so on. A mature couple will understand that friends don't need to choose between them, but immature people selfishly demand that they choose, telling them that their friendship depends on *not* being friends with the former spouse.

Understandably, friends and coworkers can play a significant role in your life while you are going through a divorce, as well as afterwards. Likewise, friends of the family can also be helpful to your children. Friends sometimes find it easier to be objective, and they can offer children an escape from their stressful home situation. Because they are not part of the family, they will not serve as reminders for children of what is happening at home.

When some children were asked, "What could other people have done to help you get through the divorce?" some of the responses were:

"Just be nice to me," said a twelve-year-old boy.

"Get my mind off it by taking me to do things," a ten-year-old girl said.

"Give encouragement," said another.

"A kind word did a lot for me," added another.

One little girl was especially fortunate: "My mom's friends became like aunts to me. We went shopping and to the movies. I could talk to them better than anyone else."

Like grandparents, aunts, and uncles, friends of Mom and Dad are frequently available to take the children on special outings or short trips. It is important for children that these long-standing relationships are maintained and that they know these people still care for them and want to be their friends. The attention of adults outside the family unit can be a stabilizing factor for a child.

What can you do to help your friends know how to respond to you, your children, and your ex-spouse during and after a divorce?

1. Be open and up front about your feelings, but *do not* subject your friends to belabored details of your divorce.

2. Ask them to be patient with you during this time of emotional upheaval. Explain that sometimes you will need to talk and other times you won't be able to.

3. Tell them that sometimes you will need to be with them and other times you need to be left alone. Ask them to be tolerant of these times and not be offended if you reject their kind offers.

4. Assure them that you understand they have a right to remain friends with both you and your ex-spouse, regardless of your relationship with your ex-spouse.

5. If appropriate, ask them to provide extra attention and support for your children, being careful to not take sides in front of the kids.

Very often others who have been through a divorce can be a good support for you because they understand your problems perhaps better than anyone else. Join one of the many support groups for people going through divorce, and make some new friends during this difficult time. How can you be a good friend to someone else who is going through a divorce?

1. Call often, but keep it brief. Let them know you are thinking about them and understand what they are going through.

2. Don't ask prying questions or give advice.

3. Don't try to top their horror story with a worse one of your own.

4. Be tactful. Don't say anything bad about their former partner.

5. Offer your companionship if they need to be with someone or just want to get away from it all.

6. Remain neutral.

7. Don't betray their confidence.

8. Work together to make new friends and develop new interests.

You, your children, and your ex-spouse need the love and support of family and friends during and after the divorce. No family should isolate itself—others help expedite the healing process. Divorce is difficult and painful, and trying to go through it without any help will only drag out that pain. By asking for assistance when you need it and offering your help to others, you will in turn be helping yourself.

I shall never forget August 1979 when I shared with my former in-laws that I was not divorcing them. I wanted them to know how important their friendship was to me. We stood by the door of my Denver home crying, hugging, and committing to being friends forever. We vowed to continue our love for one another as friends, although I would not be legally called their daughter-in-law. We have continued to send cards and letters for the past thirteen years and have made occasional visits across the country.

20

Teachers: Friends or Foes?

I hate open house at my school. My dad talks too loud to my teacher and tells her that his ex-wife won't tell him a thing about me. Everyone can hear him talk. His wife acts like she's my mom and she isn't.

Ten-year-old boy

Rachael's father filed for a divorce from her mom on the day she started kindergarten . . . a fact he did not mention to Rachael or her mother. Even though the first day of school was full of excitement and uncertainties, Rachael knew she could count on her mom to pick her up when school was over. Much to her shock and her mother's horror, when her mom arrived at the school the principal was there with a restraining order preventing Rachael's mother from taking her. Rachael's father had filed for custody and convinced the judge that her mother would attempt to steal her and leave the state once she was served with divorce papers. So a restraining order was issued by the court, preventing her mom from seeing the children without their father present until the matter was settled.

Frightened and confused, Rachael found herself in a van that was taking her to a nursery school for after-school care. Her mom was so stunned that she couldn't believe what had happened. She followed the van and tried to take her daughter home with her, but unfortunately, the nursery school also had a copy of the restraining order. They physically blocked Rachael's mother from taking her. Rachael started screaming as she watched her sobbing mother being prevented from even touching her.

Desperate to console her daughter and assure her it was all a mistake, Rachael's mom went behind the nursery school to the playground. When Rachael came out to play she saw her mother and came running to her. They grabbed hands through the openings in the wire fence and clung to each other. As soon as the attendants saw what was happening, they grabbed a screaming Rachael and pried her hands away from her tearful mother.

Rachael, her mother, the teachers, the principal, and the nursery school staff were put in an unfortunate position by a vindictive father who did not consider what effect his actions would have on his daughter. Rachael perceived her teachers at kindergarten and at the nursery school as her enemies because they wouldn't allow her to see her mom. After all, she never had this problem until she started kindergarten.

Although very skillful at exercising power and acting out his anger, Rachael's father was unable to have compassion for her and consider her best interests. Not only did she had a perfect right to be with her mother after school, but she needed to view her teachers as neutral parties rather than cruel people who kept her away from her mother. After six months of legal hassles, Rachael's mother regained custody and convinced the judge she did not intend to steal Rachael and take her out of state. Although she won the legal battle, she lost six precious months of being with her daughter . . . time lost forever.

Unfortunately, many parents deliberately sabotage their child's happiness and post-divorce adjustment by not cooperating with the other parent on the basics that pertain to a child's welfare. School is a crucial element in that adjustment.

If at all possible, don't allow your children's teachers to be caught in the middle. Your children need to perceive their teacher as a neutral, stable party who is consistently there for them, rather than one who enforces Dad's rules or takes Mom's side.

Kyle and Jill were awarded joint custody of their children, which implied a cordial arrangement and technically allowed the children to have optimal time with each parent and the parents to have equal involvement in the kids' lives. Every two weeks the children lived with a different parent. Each parent, however, sought devious ways to keep the other uninformed of what was happening in the children's lives. Their son, Chris, had an exceptionally high IQ, but his grades were rapidly sliding into the failure range. Note after note went home to Jill, but she chose to use it in her battle against Kyle rather than consider Chris's academic welfare.

When Kyle came to open house, he was shocked that Chris was failing some subjects. This was the first time he had heard of any trouble. Furious with the teacher that he hadn't been told, Kyle was shown notes that she had sent home, along with their dates. Each of the notes had been sent when the children were staying with their mother.

Jill tried to use the incident as ammunition against Kyle, opening up the custody hearing again and telling the court that he did not care about the children's welfare and did not make them study. Kyle told the court that Jill refused to communicate with him about how the children were doing in school. Each openly criticized the other in front of the children. It is no wonder that Chris's grades reached the danger point and that both the children developed nervous tics, started wetting the bed, and began displaying the classic symptoms of depression.

Even if parents and extended family are cooperative and totally supportive of a child, the trauma of divorce will still affect a child's performance at school. Children of divorce frequently have a drop in academic performance. Often a lack of structure at home and worries over financial insecurity result in emotional instability that leads to trouble in the classroom. These factors, coupled with the emotional stress of the parents, make it difficult for a child to keep his or her mind on schoolwork.

Here is just a brief list of some of the problems these children face.

- Mondays and Fridays are very difficult because the children are trying to adjust to the transition between parents.
- Parents frequently get into fights when picking up or dropping off the children. This is very upsetting to the kids.
- Mom might be away from home and working for the first time. The child might have to get ready for school without a parent present or come home to an empty house.
- The family income and standard of living might have dropped considerably.
- Schoolwork becomes less important than dealing with the emotions of the divorce.
- Children have a sudden drop in self-esteem.

Some typical behaviors that teachers have noticed among these children include:

- Short attention spans
- Daydreaming and fantasizing
- Weariness or nervousness
- A drop in grades
- Alienation from fellow students
- A tendency to cling to teachers

Due to the working parent's schedule, children of divorce often lack structure at home. And because some children have to get ready for school without the supervision of Mom or Dad, they wind up looking uncared for—unbathed, wearing dirty clothing, and arriving late.

Many of them are also teased by other children, which alienates them even more.

Current studies estimate that 25 percent of school-age children are living in single-parent homes. Teachers must then function as second parents to many of their students. Since most kids spend more time in the classroom than at home, school becomes their second home. Children with an unsettled home situation often look to the teacher to be that reliable, constant source of security, and they count on that teacher being there every day from 9 to 3. This often offers more certainty than anything that happens at home because some children may not know if they will see Mom or Dad that night. If the parents are dating, there may be a stranger in the home or a baby-sitter if the parent goes out. But the teacher's presence in the classroom never changes except for an occasional substitute. Children often depend on that security; and it is impossible to separate their emotional life from their academic life.

Studies have shown that children of single-parent families differ in eleven areas from children of those in two-parent families. These are:

1. More tardiness
2. Achievement (some students' grades dropped and others improved in an attempt to bring the other parent back home)
3. Greater number of absences from school
4. Greater number of health clinic visits
5. Greater number of discipline referrals
6. Greater number of suspensions
7. Greater number of days suspended
8. Greater number of free lunches
9. Greater number of reduced-price lunches
10. Greater number of children with government funding
11. Greater number of children transferred[1]

Having children in the classroom who are going through the trauma of divorce puts an added burden on teachers. Not only are those students usually more difficult to teach at this time, but there are problems dealing with the parents.

While Kyle and Jill's fierce custody battle was raging, the kids became behavior problems in the classroom, reverting to infantile behavior. The teachers called the parents in individually for a talk, but all each of them did was complain about their soon-to-be ex-spouse and blame the other for their children's problems.

Rather than tone down their wild incriminations in front of the children, they put the teachers into the battle also. Each parent had the teachers served with subpoenas to testify against the other parent.

Ultimately, a child's problems at home have repercussions for the teacher. Some children are compliant at home out of regard for the difficulties their parents are experiencing, but they act out their frustrations at school by becoming aggressive toward classmates, bullying, and acting bossy.

Teachers can play a significant role in the healing process *if* they are aware of the situation and are asked to help. Notify your children's teachers as soon as possible about the divorce and discuss the following with them:

1. Tell them what's going on in your children's lives so that they can deal more effectively with their problems.

2. Ask them to pay extra attention to your kids during this time, if at all possible.

3. Explain that they may see changing behavior patterns that may not be positive.

4. Ask them to let your kids know if there is a special time set aside each day when they are available to help or talk in private.

5. Tell them your children might need a little more reassurance than normal—even just patting them on the shoulder—and you would appreciate any extra affection or special attention they could offer.

6. Ask them to try not to refer to illustrations about

the family as just being the nuclear family, but explain that there are many different types of families and living arrangements. Make sure children understand there is nothing to be ashamed of if they are from a divorced home.

7. Ask them to allow the children to express their feelings about divorce during appropriate times. For example, make divorce one of the topics for a writing or art assignment.

8. Ask if the school district has social workers, school psychologists, or other counselors who are available to assist your children, if necessary.

9. Ask if the school district offers the children any special programs on divorce. Many do.

10. Ask the teachers to be a little more compassionate with your kids while they are going through the divorce. Tell the teacher you feel it will help minimize discipline problems if they are given special assignments and responsibilities that place them in the role of a leader and increase their self-esteem. For example, being in charge of passing out papers, deciding what goes on a bulletin board for a week, or some activity appropriate to their age.

11. Tell them that you feel all the above actions will help the children perform better in the classroom. By finding a positive outlet for their pent-up frustrations, they will be better able to concentrate on their school work.

12. Ask them to be willing to schedule two parent-teacher conferences for your children if your ex-spouse will not attend the conference with you. Emphasize the importance of both parents being informed about their children's activities and progress.

A growing number of schools are developing programs to deal with the problems unique to these kids since such a large percentage of children are involved. If your school district does not now offer such a program but is interested, please have them contact me at the address in the back of this book. I present a program in schools called "Children Facing Divorce" and spend one-and-a-half days with children who are going through divorce or who have experienced a divorce in the past ten years. This is funded by the PTA, the Principal's Fund, and school districts.

21

I wish someone would tell my dad to get rid of his girlfriend and her kids and pay a little attention to me.

Twelve-year-old girl

A Child's Perception of Dating

Most experts agree that a sufficient grieving period—usually between two and five years—be allowed before remarrying. These days, when many people are postponing marriage to establish a career, it is highly likely that the person you or your ex-spouse chooses to marry has absolutely no experience with children. Under these circumstances, the new relationship will need all the help it can get, and it doesn't need the excess emotional baggage of a crew of grief-stricken children who haven't been permitted time to recover from the divorce. The following are some tips that can make this stage a little easier.

Explain to your children that adults need time for fun too. When your kids first hear that you are going to be seeing someone other than Dad or Mom, they may not understand. You may suddenly start working out, wearing different clothes, wearing makeup, and doing your hair differently because you're starting over, but to your children you may look like a stranger. While younger children may nod and understand once they know what's going on, this can be especially hard on teens, who never have thought of you as a sexual being—you are simply Mom or Dad. Having you act like or mistaken for their brother or sister can be disconcerting.

Various things that young adults have said indicate that their parents' dating or sex life had a traumatic effect on their lives. They either became promiscuous themselves, mirroring their parents' activity, or they reversed their parents' new lifestyle by breaking off all relationships with the opposite sex.

The young adults surveyed were most staggered by the apparent moral reversals in their parents' behavior. In stunned disbelief, a twenty-year-old woman discovered her "buttoned up, Bible carrying" mother in bed with a man two years older than her son. Another student witnessed his ambitious, seemingly conscience-ridden father walk away from his family and his lucrative law firm for destinations unknown. As though looking through lenses badly out of focus, many gazed upon parents they no longer recognized and struggled over which image was false, which authentic.

"Was the old Mom just hiding under the real one that is coming out now?" a twenty-one-year-old man wondered. "Was that tender, loving person all a lie? Was I just not seeing what I didn't want to see? And if that's true, then how am I supposed to trust what I think I see now?"[1]

Keep your child informed. Nobody likes to be left in the dark, least of all a child. Your social life, which may be critical to your happiness, must not eclipse your obligation to let your child know what you're up to. *The Kids' Book of Divorce*, a small book written by children with the help of Eric Rofes as editor, puts it this way:

Not knowing what is going on is one of the worst things that can probably happen. How would you feel if the parent you've living with tells you that he or she is going out for a few hours with some friends and leaves you at home by yourself and doesn't come back until morning? Do you think this is fair?[2]

You may think that this doesn't happen very often or, if it does, only in lower socio-economic homes. Unfortunately, *many* single mothers with children can't afford baby-sitters. Many of the young children surveyed who lived in middle-class homes before the divorce reported that after they went to bed, their mothers left them home alone while they went out on dates. One eight-year-old boy said, "I woke up at two in the morning and my mom still wasn't home from her date. I called Grandma's house, but she didn't answer the phone, so I decided to walk to Grandma's because I didn't want to be alone. Grandma only lived four miles away, but a policeman saw me and took me over to Grandma's. Then everyone got mad at Mom."

Other children reported that they hated breakfast more than any other time of the day because they never knew if one of Mom's dates was going to be having breakfast with them. Can you imagine a child's shock at having a strange man sitting across the breakfast table? What kind of stable environment is that? Or of a little girl coming home from summer camp to find Mommy waiting in her car with her new husband? You need to reassure your children that if your relationship with a particular friend becomes serious, they'll be the first to know.

Be honest. Make sure that the information you give your children is as accurate and as clearly explained as possible. Imagine the misinformation this child was given: "I don't want a 'big brother.' My dad might find out and then he wouldn't be my dad anymore." Some children truly fear that a stepparent will forever blot out the memory of a natural parent. Be certain your child knows that Dad will always be Dad and Mom will always be Mom.

There is a balance to be achieved in how much you tell your children, however. There is no need to inform the child of every move you make or every date you go on, lest he become accustomed to granting you "permission." A general description of your plans and a time when you'll be home should be sufficient.

Don't parade your dates in front of your children— either before or after the divorce. Ginny was only six when her father started using her as a cover to go see his girlfriends before her mother divorced him. When he told her mother he and Ginny were going out for a while, the mom would always say, "Don't let her have any sweets between meals." As soon as they left the house the dad would offer to buy her a hot fudge sundae . . . which she dearly loved. Then they would go over to his girlfriend's house and tell Ginny to stay in the kitchen and eat her sundae or watch TV while Daddy went to see his sick friend in the bedroom. Afterward, he would tell Ginny, "I won't tell Mommy you had a hot fudge sundae if you won't tell Mommy we came to see my friend. She would be mad at both of us." Although few are as blatant about it as Ginny's father, some parents are totally insensitive to their children's feelings or how they will react years later as they look back and understand what was happening.

When you start dating, arrange to meet your dates elsewhere or try to limit your dating to those times when the children are with the other parent. The people who are most successful at protecting their children and their dates from unwarranted worry or hostility never allow their children to meet their date and do not give out their home phone number to dates. They insist on being called at work or contacted through a friend.

Until you are fairly serious about someone, there is no sense in exposing your children to this person. The kids may hate the date, act like monsters to alienate the person, be afraid, or begin to form some emotional attachment that might be abruptly cut off . . . only to be renewed each time another date comes over.

Seeing their parents with someone else can be quite

upsetting to some children. "Mom kisses her boy-friend," said one child. "I hate it. He's not my dad." Said one girl, "I don't know why my mom needs a boy-friend. One stepparent in the family is enough."

There is a funny but sad cartoon of a child who has been exposed too many times to Mom's boyfriends standing in front of the couch, addressing Mother and friend. The caption reads: "I don't want to put you on the spot, but do you think your living arrangement will last long enough to invest in a bike for me?"[3]

Once a relationship becomes serious, it is important to start gradually working this individual into the children's lives.

If the commitment was the cause of the divorce, don't assume the children are stupid. Steve was anxious for his divorce to be final so he could marry Casandra. Although he had limited time with his children, he never wanted to go anyplace without her. During each visit he would make elaborate preparations to have a group of people with them at all times for picnics, parties, or trips to fun places. Casandra was always in the group as a friend of someone else. Steve thought the kids were unaware of his relationship, but all they had to do was watch the way their dad looked at her. It caused the children to be hostile to both Casandra and Steve. They couldn't believe their dad thought they were so dumb. One day fourteen-year-old Tim walked up to the friend who had supposedly brought Casandra and said, "Tell Dad he isn't fooling us. We get to see him two days a month. Couldn't he just be with us? He has all the rest of the month to be with Casandra. We don't even get to talk to him without a group of people around."

Avoid using your children as spies, grilling them for information on your ex-spouse's new life. Consider the following exchange between a mother and her son, who has just come back from a weekend at Dad's:

"Did you have fun yesterday, Joey?" asks Mom.

"Yeah. We went to the park and Debbie pushed me on the swings."

"Debbie? Who's she?"

"Oh, she's just Dad's new girlfr . . . ," says Joey, realizing he's said too much.

"Oh really? What does she look like? Where did Dad meet her? Did she buy you anything?"

And Dad might be doing the same thing at his house. It doesn't take long for children to realize they are pawns in a cruel game between parents, and they'll clam up. This parental inquisition can go on for years if left unchecked.

When you do become serious about someone new, introduce your children to the person and arrange to do something together (preferably a children's activity) before you tell them about it. Once you decide to remarry, inform the children while they are alone with you. Don't do it in front of your significant other. Timing is important here.

22

> When I had a stepdad, I loved him probably more than my real dad because he was there when we needed him. That divorce hurt as much as the first one.
> Thirteen-year-old boy

His, Hers, and Ours . . . The Stepfamily

THE CHILD'S VIEWPOINT

A quick look in the dictionary reveals that the words *stepmother, stepfather, stepchild*—or *stepanyone* for that matter—are derived from the Old English prefix "steop," meaning bereaved of children, bereaved children, or orphans, depending on its use. In that day, when divorce was largely unheard of and disease was rampant, stepparents were acquired when someone had *died*. Life in the latter half of the twentieth century has changed all that.

For several years now, experts have been saying that in the 1990s more people will be part of a second marriage than a first marriage. With such annexation of new fathers, mothers, siblings, grandparents, and cousins at an ever-increasing rate, it's clear that there is a need for the natural parents to keep a level head and make such transitions as smooth as possible for their children. These days, typically nobody has died, and you as a parent are likely emerging from a fairly painful separation from your spouse. The harsh feelings left over from such a traumatic experience can cause some people to consider some pretty vicious courses of action. And these feelings may only get worse when your ex-spouse, or even you, finds someone new.

According to an article in *Reader's Digest*,

> The impact of remarriage on a family, no matter how high the expectations, is second only to the crisis of divorce. Because there are no guidelines for acceptable stepfamily behavior, at least one expert attributes the higher rate of divorce in second marriages . . . to the strain of trying to work it all out.

> Children entering a stepfamily can feel twice defeated, once for having been unable to prevent the divorce, and again for not being able to prevent the remarriage. The stepparent may bear the brunt of anger the children have stored up toward the parent they feel deserted them. To add to the confusion, children of remarriage often inherit an instant set of stepsisters and stepbrothers, relationships they are not prepared for.[1]

Laurie's father (yes, the same Laurie who burned the bacon in Chapter 13) lived about fifteen miles from Laurie and her mother. She visited him every other weekend. Although Laurie loved her father, she resented his girlfriend, Susan, who always interfered with her visits and conversations with her dad. He could see Susan any time; Laurie's visits were her special time with her father and she wanted him alone.

Laurie arrived at her father's house one Saturday morning looking forward to a good time together when he dropped an emotional bomb on her. "Susan and I got married last weekend, so now you have two mothers. We want you to call her 'Mom' or 'Mother,' and we will all be one happy family . . . you, me, 'Mom,' and her son, Jeff, who is now your stepbrother."

No one had considered Laurie's feelings. She could have been informed privately by her father in advance of the wedding. How dare he betray her like this? Now this weird guy named Jeff would be living with her dad all the time. He would get attention that belonged to her. Shocked and furious, Laurie screamed, "I hate you . . . all of you . . . she will never be my mom!" Crying frantically and in need of love and reassurance, Laurie stormed out of the house.

Spotting Jeff's bike, Laurie picked it up and started riding without caring where she was going. She just wanted to get away. Never had she felt so miserable, lonely, unwanted, and unloved. Sometimes she rode and cried. Other times she stopped and cried. Mostly she just cried. What was left of her heart was smashed to bits.

It was dark when the policeman noticed Laurie sitting on the curb with the bike beside her. He could see where the tears had left clean streaks down her dirty face. Laurie refused to give him her name, address, or phone number. She just kept repeating, "Nobody loves me, *nobody*!"

Several hours later the police connected her father's missing child report with Laurie and called him to come get her. At first Laurie refused to go home with her dad, but when she found out her mother had left town for the weekend, she didn't have much choice.

Respecting Laurie's feelings and telling her of the marriage in advance of the wedding might have prevented much of the trauma and shock she experienced. Gradually working Susan and Jeff into the picture would not have been as devastating for her. Laurie's behavior problems increased as her self-worth diminished.

Consider the stereotypical image of the stepmother, for example. Throughout history, everyone from Mother Goose to the Brothers Grimm has nurtured the image of the stepmother as a purveyor of discord, aggression, hatred, and poison apples. Children, of course, know about Cinderella and Hansel and Gretel, and these storybook images, added to their natural inclination to protect the unity of their family, work against either parent trying to bring someone new into the fold. Witnessed by her children, a mother's backbiting, vengeful attitude toward her ex-husband and his new love does nothing but exacerbate these misconceptions, possibly causing permanent emotional damage to the child.

Just the anticipation of getting stepparents can be negative for a child. A thirteen-year-old girl answered the survey question, "If you have stepparents, how do you feel about them?" with "I don't have any, but if I did, I wouldn't feel comfortable at all."

Both parents can promote healthy, productive relationships among all concerned parties, keeping the welfare of the children uppermost in mind. In this chapter, we will attempt to draw the parent out of his or her shell of hurt and turmoil, and reveal some of the ways kids are hurting, how they feel, and how to help when a parent—custodial or non-custodial—begins a new relationship and possibly remarries.

There is no such thing as a generic child, and therefore there is no such thing as a generic reaction to the introduction of a new love interest or spouse. Kids' feelings, ranging from jealousy and insecurity about this new person, to guilt and disloyalty to the natural parent for liking him or her, will vary depending on how much discord there was in the previous marriage, how cooperative the parents are, how gregarious the child is, and countless other factors. Some children even express relief that their parents are moving on with their lives.

One teen expressed his desire for a stepparent: "I would like to see my dad get married again and settle down."

While speaking of the needs of children of divorce, Kathleen L. Kircher, executive director of the North American Conference of Separated/Divorced Catholics, said,

Teenagers open up and let their guts out, but then there is no follow-up on what they have revealed. Children often keep their emotions bottled up, not wanting to add to the burdens they believe their custodial parents already shoulder. Perhaps it is the lack of expression of feelings such as anger and grief which in turn creates so many problems when the child becomes part of a remarriage family. Certainly the statistics show that remarriage families are more likely to end in divorce than first marriages.[2]

A parent would be wise to be in touch not only with his or her own feelings, but also with those of the children involved and with the reality of just how powerful their feelings might be.

In an article in the *Marriage and Divorce Today Newsletter*, Greta W. Stanton, an associate professor at Rutgers University and director of the Step Center for Stepfamily Consultation and Education, said:

A stepfamily is a family born out of the losses endured by each family member: the child has lost a parent, at least one parent has lost a partner and even a previously unmarried stepparent has lost the dream of a nuclear family. However, on the remarriage of one parent, custodial or not, the loss is greatest to the child. The parent has or at least hopes to have a positive new life experience. For the child, however, not only does the remarriage put an end to the dream of parental reunion (in the case of divorce), but it is also supposed to be an occasion for joy for the child, as well as for the re-wed parent.[3]

For many children, however, the idea of a new parent is a cause for anything but joy. Some parents include their children in the marriage ceremony to the new spouse. According to the children, this is quite traumatic for them.

A thirteen-year-old girl said, "I cried for two hours before the ceremony the day my dad and stepmom got married. I told them it was because I just got my ears pierced and they still hurt, but I was crying because I knew my mother was home crying."

Ten-year-old Jacob was a candlelighter in his dad's big church wedding three months after his parents' divorce. Although he told his dad he was happy for him, Jacob's own grief caused him to sob openly all during the ceremony, even though he had to remain on the platform in a white dinner jacket and endure the picture-taking session afterward. Later, Jacob told his mother, "It was just as sad as Grandma's funeral. I knew it meant we could never all be together again as a family."

Most recent evidence indicates that it's hard for children to adjust to a stepparent for at least the first two years of the new marriage even when there has been sufficient time to recover from the divorce. Said one sixteen-year-old girl, "My stepfather gets on my nerves bad!" "My dad's wife is kind of a witch," said another. "We don't talk much." One child put it succinctly: "I hate my stepmonster." There is simply so much going on, so much to get used to. Exercising the ultimate in self-control when asked how he felt about his stepmother, a twelve-year-old boy said: "No comment."

Children are asking themselves, "Can I trust this person? Will this person leave me? Does my parent really like this person? Does he or she really like me? Does he or she really like my parent?"

"I hated my stepmom," wrote one twelve-year-old girl, "but when she left my dad and took my half sister, I began to miss them. Now I love her."

A seventeen-year-old boy wrote: "I used to dislike my stepfather, but I'm beginning to accept him now."

Many other kids also expressed ambivalent feelings:

"I have a stepmother, and I don't really know her; but what I do know of her I don't like."

"I feel a little insecure when I am around my stepmom."

"My stepdad is real strict. My stepmom is understanding, but sometimes she loses her temper."

"I love my stepmom, but sometimes I hate my stepdad."

"I used to have a stepparent and I liked him . . . but then again I didn't."

In her book *In the Middle*, author Mary Kehle demonstrates just how hard adjusting to a new life can be:

> Melissa not only had to get used to a new stepbrother and sister, she also had a new stepfather. Since her natural father was still living nearby, Melissa was confused at times. She seemed to have two fathers, each telling her what to do. She didn't mind too much when her dad made her behave. But when Bob, her stepfather, tried to correct her, she got mad and resentful. "You're not my dad," she would say. "I don't have to listen to you."

> But other times when Bob did things with his own daughter and son, Melissa felt jealous and left out. She wanted him to pay attention to her. And when he did, like the times he sat and played Scrabble with her, she really enjoyed it. It was so confusing![4]

As has been mentioned before, 90 percent of the time the mother becomes custodial parent. Since this is so often the case, the most typical problem is that of a child having to become accustomed to a non-custodial father's new wife. A portion of an article titled, "Stepmothers: Image of Wickedness, Casualty of the Fractured Family," by *Washington Post* writer Megan Rosenfeld, seems appropriate:

> While a stepmother may see herself as a phoenix rising from the ashes of a dead marriage to create a new life, the children see her as symbol of their destroyed home. She represents their hurt, the fact that their father isn't

living with them anymore, or the death of their mother. No matter what the child's age is, whether three or thirty, resistance is almost inevitable. This resistance ("acting out" in psychiatric parlance) can range from reserve to rudeness to more brutal forms like getting involved with drugs, running away, or wrecking a car.[5]

This "acting out," as mentioned by Rosenfeld, can take various forms. One common activity practiced by the more creative children of divorce is to take advantage of the competitiveness exhibited by feuding parents and stepparents. "It is one thing to 'butter up' people in childhood to gain an end," says Linda Bird Francke in her book, *Growing Up Divorced*, "But children of divorce and remarriage truly become expert at the devious game of manipulation and artfully play one parent off against the other."[6] Francke cites a case where a college student, in need of money, wrote two letters requesting funds—one to his dad, in which he complains about his stepfather; and one to his stepfather, in which he complains about his dad. He got money from both. Another little girl bragged to her stepmother about how her natural mother bought her ice cream and took her to the movies. She was soon on her way to the theater.

And all of this can be going on while Mom is telling her kids how Hansel and Gretel's wicked stepmother forced their father to abandon them in the woods.

Conflict existing between the ex-spouse and the new spouse drastically affects the child's perception of the new stepparent. A nine-year-old girl said, "I think I could like my stepmother better if my mommy didn't hate her so much."

Overcoming the animosity and winning the approval of the children is an uphill battle at best. Many children, however, are very warm toward one stepparent and cool toward the other, depending upon which parent they perceive as being "dumped."

A sixteen-year-old boy whose dad left his mom for

another woman said, "My dad's wife is kind of a witch. We don't talk much. But my mom's new husband is cool. We're pretty good friends. He doesn't try to take my dad's place."

Likewise, an eighteen-year-old girl whose dad also left for another woman said, "I dislike my stepmother very much and not because of jealousy. I love my stepfather very much; we are good friends."

Though certainly not one of the happier times of a child's life, all experiences during this tumultuous phase need not be negative. At a meeting of the New York chapter of the Stepfamily Association of America, parents were surprised to learn that many kids believed that the remarriage of one or both parents need not be overly traumatic.[7] During a question-and-answer session between parents and kids, it was revealed that one of the biggest problems holding a child back from emotional recovery is the guilt they feel when they develop an attachment to a stepparent. The children stressed that having fun with stepparents doesn't lessen their feelings for their parents. "It's not like one is taking the place of the other," said one girl. "They're both totally different people you can enjoy in different ways."

One of the healthiest responses to our questionnaire about stepfamilies came from Leah, a fifteen-year-old girl: "I don't even remember when my parents divorced because I was only four, but I like having three sets of brothers and sisters. I have my real sister, a stepbrother and stepsister from my stepdad, and a stepbrother and stepsister from my stepmother. They are all *totally* different and it helps me learn about different lifestyles and decide what kind I want."

Indeed, many children grow quite fond of the new additions to their families. "I have a stepfather and he's the greatest thing in the world," remarked one seventeen-year-old. "I love them [stepparents] as if they were my own," commented another.

Other positive comments included:

"I love my stepmother."

"She is really fun."

"He is nice to me, and I like him and consider him my real dad."

"I love my stepfather more than anyone! He can't ever be on the same level as my real father. He most definitely passes him by."

While children do require much tender loving care, their resiliency and adaptability must never be underestimated. One child expressed his ability to integrate his feelings for his stepparent this way: "I have one stepparent. I like him. He is also a good person. It is kind of like having three parents."

23

Forgiveness is the answer
to the child's dream of a
miracle by which what
is broken is made whole
again.[1]
Dag Hammarskjöld

Forgiveness: The
Ultimate Healer

My D-day was June 1, 1979, our anniversary. I was looking forward to a fun evening out to celebrate sixteen
wonderful years of marriage when my husband, Larry,
came home. Instead of bringing me flowers, he brought
me the news that he wanted a divorce. Dumb? Stupid?
Naïve? Yes, maybe I was all those and more, but I had
not thought that divorce could happen to me. We were
the ideal family . . . weren't we? I thought we had it all—
a loving marriage, a collie name Felice, a beautiful two-
story dream house, a two-car garage with an automatic
door opener, and even a trash compactor. Our greatest
assets, however, were Cheri, our twelve-year-old daughter, and Brad, our eight-year-old son.

Shock and numbness set in. I was unable to function.
It seemed like the end of the world . . . it was the end
of my world as I knew it.

During a cold, rainy, dreary afternoon in November
1979 while my children were visiting their father, I lay
on the sofa in the family room in a state of depression.
Tears rolled down my cheeks as I stared through the window at the gray clouds. *What will happen to me? Where
am I to go? What is my purpose for living?* I wondered
to myself.

A voice from deep inside said, "What do you want to do?" (It's funny how those voices come at perfect moments!)

I thought, *I want to move to Phoenix and teach children.*

In June 1980, after moving to Phoenix and four months after my legal divorce, I drove to San Diego, California, for two weeks to evaluate my life and think about what I would do and be for the next fifty years. My future looked bleak and hopeless. How could I exist without my ex-husband, with whom I had shared my life for nearly twenty years?

When I arrived at the beach, I took off my sneakers, stretched out my towel, made a little seat in the sand, reached in my knapsack for a copy of *The Greatest Miracle in the World* by Og Mandino, and began reading.

The sun was hot, the water cold. I was numb. Several hours later the sun was dropping into the ocean, the waves were lapping at my feet, and tears were rolling down my cheeks as I read:

For how could one improve on a miracle? You were a marvel to behold and I was pleased. I gave you this world and dominion over it. Then, to enable you to reach your full potential I placed my hand upon you, once more, and endowed you with powers unknown to any other creature in the universe, even unto this day.

> I gave you the power to think.
> I gave you the power to love.
> I gave you the power to will.
> I gave you the power to laugh.
> I gave you the power to imagine.
> I gave you the power to create.
> I gave you the power to plan.
> I gave you the power to speak.
> I gave you the power to pray.

My pride in you knows no bounds. You were my ultimate creation, my greatest miracle. A complete living being. One who can adjust to any climate, any hardship, any challenge. One who can manage his own destiny without any interference from me. One who can translate a sensation or perception, not by instinct, but by thought and deliberation into whatever action is best for himself and all humanity.

I cried to myself—*Me a miracle? How?* My self-esteem had hit bottom. What could I possibly do to reach my full potential? Did I even have potential? Somehow I *knew* it was all true . . . I am the greatest miracle. I do have a purpose. I *knew* it would be OK. I would make it.

It took time, though. And help. I honestly don't know how anyone makes it through a divorce without professional help. I sought support through my divorce disaster from a psychologist friend, Ken Magid, Ph.D. He told me, "Laurene, you have all the oil in the Middle East in the palm of your hand right now; you just don't know it yet. But you will."

I had to spend the next couple of years grieving before I knew the truth of his words. We all have the rich oil of our unique gifts and talents within us, but many times we aren't aware of it until after a crisis.

Three years later, I held on to that knowledge, and through God's guidance and my faith, I began the "Children of Divorce" and "Successful Living after Divorce" programs in Scottsdale, Arizona. Through my own pain I began helping others—parents and children—survive their own personal earthquake.

I have been specializing in children of divorce and single parenting in my private practice. In 1986, I began an international tour, speaking to children of divorce (and about them to other professionals) in many countries, including Japan and the USSR. Sharing, giving, and receiving information on how to work with them was a dream from deep within. An unexpected side effect of helping others through divorce was that it also helped me put my situation into perspective.

I want to thank Og Mandino for his gift to me. He helped me realize that I could adjust to any situation, any challenge, just as you can. What I didn't realize until much later was that of all the powers we are given, one of the most powerful is the power to forgive. After a few years I began to think of my ex-husband *and his wife* as my friends. Sometimes it takes years, but when it happens, the miracle of reconciliation has a profound healing effect on a broken family. Here's how it happened in our family . . .

GUESS WHO CAME TO DINNER?

After my sixteen-year-old son, Brad, invited his father and his wife to Thanksgiving dinner, I began to get butterflies.

They say it takes half as long for the survivor to heal as the marriage was long. Sixteen divided by two equals eight. How did "they" know the formula? This was the ninth Thanksgiving we had been apart. My healing process had been gradual, and sometimes I felt I was a slow learner.

Never before had we all been together by choice, with love and caring, let alone shared a meal. Our twenty-year-old daughter, Cheri, would be home from college for the holidays, and I had also invited my eighty-year-old mother, Wilma Hansen, as well as my significant other, at that time Brian, and his son, Brian, Jr.

My kids were excited. We told Cheri about the invitation over the telephone. She yelled to her roommate, "Guess what, my parents are eating together on Thanksgiving!" Cheri said she was shocked and never dreamed her mother and father would ever again be together on Thanksgiving.

My kids may have been excited, but I was panicking.

Even though my ex-husband, Larry, was our travel agent and seemed to like Brian, I was concerned. What would we do after dinner? What would we talk about? A friend suggested playing Pictionary—a game something like charades except players draw pictures rather than act.

When Larry and his wife, Cathy, arrived, everyone else was present. As soon as they walked into the house, Cathy gave me a hug and said, "Happy Thanksgiving!" I felt the warmth and excitement of a long-overdue healing beginning.

We all did our own thing until dinner. Cathy stirred the gravy, Brian carved the turkey. Larry joked with Cheri, Brad, and Brian, Jr. Mother and Cheri discussed the wedding dress my mother had made me in 1963—the same dress Cheri had worn for her sorority initiation. Believe it or not, Cheri brought out some old pictures of Larry and me from 1960 to 1970. I was feeling uncomfortable with Cathy watching. I felt for her because she wasn't part of those old pictures. That was my first clue that I felt unconditional love for Cathy. I was surprised at my feelings.

Everyone was seated in pairs, with mother at the head of the table and Larry and Cathy across from Brian and me. We all joined hands and closed our eyes. Brad and Brian, Jr., grinned and giggled nervously at each other. Brian prayed. I'll never forget it.

"Dear God, thank You for our family being present today on Thanksgiving. Thank You for the love we share. Help each one of us stay on the purpose You have for us. Thank You for Your gift of forgiveness." My heart stopped with that word, and there was a long pause before he began again. "Be with all those not present: Erin [his daughter], Joyce [Brian, Jr.'s, mother], Jimmy [Cathy's nineteen-year-old son], and all our loved ones, and also family who are no longer living. May we have a joyous day of celebration. In Jesus' name, Amen."

Cheri said, "This is the first Thanksgiving in nine years I haven't had to eat two turkeys." We all laughed.

We toasted to "good friends," and everyone complimented each other's food. No one told inside jokes. Or if they did, they included everyone in it. The children were thrilled to have both Mom and Dad at the same holiday table.

I looked across the table a couple of times, trying to believe this was real. I even tried to remember that first Thanksgiving when the kids and I were all alone. Even that didn't bring up painful feelings. Was this real? I said to myself, *Laurene, do you know who that is across the table? That's your ex and his wife. What do you think about that?*

Afterward we all cleaned up. Brian was at the sink, Cheri brought out Pictionary, and we started playing. There were a couple of marginally obscene words in the game where we all blushed. Brian turned red. "What did your mother think? What would Larry and Cathy think?" For the next three hours we laughed, joked, and yelled as we tried to beat the one-minute timer. Even my mother threw her hands up in fun. She had supported me through the divorce, and I wondered if she also felt disbelief about the entire day.

As the evening concluded, my mother grew tired. Everyone began leaving. Cathy and I hugged. Larry hugged Mother and gave her a kiss of goodwill on the cheek. He gave me a hug with a big smile of thanks.

Then I knew the secret. *Forgiveness* is the ultimate healer. Charles Stanley defined forgiveness as "the act of setting someone free from an obligation to you that is a result of a wrong done against you."[2] Although I felt a wrong had been done to me, I was able to release my ex-husband from any obligations I felt he owed me. For the first time since our divorce, I could see him as a separate entity, a vulnerable person with unfulfilled needs and dreams of his own.

I also realized that with forgiveness comes unconditional love. I discovered this several months later when I felt some disappointment and sadness for my ex-husband as he shared about some big changes in his career. As he left, I felt sad for him. I realized I did love him unconditionally—not as a husband but as a child of God. I wanted only the best for him and for his dreams to come true.

Forgiveness and reconciliation as friends and parents has made the divorce so much easier on our children. We now share graduations and holidays without the children worrying about not being able to invite both Mom and Dad to the same occasion.

As I stood next to Larry on the bleachers at Brad's high school graduation, I couldn't resist any longer. I took a small step to my right, put my arm around his waist, looked up at him and said, "Well, we did it."

He responded quickly and without hesitancy with a tight hug, leaned down toward me and said, "Good job, Mom."

"Good job, Dad," I responded with tears falling down my cheeks.

For ten years I had dreamed and fantasized about receiving some kind of confirmation from Larry regarding my successful single-parenting skills. I now had a new realization of what I really wanted from Larry. It wasn't to be told how hard I had worked to raise our two children alone for ten years, not the sacrifice, but instead a confirmation that we were two human beings doing the best we could with the awareness and understanding we had at the time, both of us loving and giving to our children in our own way.

Most single parents never receive any affirmation from either their ex-spouse or their children. I was fortunate that not only did I receive it from my ex-husband, but also from my daughter, who asked me to be a guest speaker on single parenting for her sociology class at Northern Arizona University. Ten minutes before I was to speak, she finished her talk on single parenting and drew a picture on the board. She said, "My mom is a supermom—she's a single parent—she's everything to everyone, especially Brad and me.'' She drew a stick figure wearing running shoes, holding a broom in one hand (housekeeper) and a brief case in the other (career mother). The torso consisted of one big heart. Around the stick figure she had a skillet (cook), a book (taking care of intellectual needs), a cross (representing spiritual commitment and church), and ''PTA.''

It was one of those moments parents wait a lifetime for . . . some affirmation from your child that you did a pretty good job. I immediately choked up with tears and could hardly get up to give my speech. I was amazed that she had forgiven my mistakes so completely, that she *had* seen me as a good mother.

When I suggest to my clients the importance of forgiving their ex-spouse, I sometimes see a look of horror on their faces. I can see they haven't healed yet, and more time must elapse before I suggest it again. This is a good barometer of their healing process.

One of the most incredible examples I've ever heard of a wife forgiving her husband involved a man who left his wife of sixteen years and married a sixteen-year-old girl he had gotten pregnant. After the child was born, the young mother decided she didn't want to be bothered with a baby. When the man's ex-wife heard about it from her son, she offered to take the child and raise it for them. Unbelievable as it all seems, they allowed her to raise the child as her own. She not only had forgiven her husband, but she loved him enough to want to raise his child by the young girl, rather than see it receive inadequate care.

Unfortunately, most of us get stuck in some strong emotions that fall far short of forgiveness. If you are still unable to forgive your former spouse and have a cordial relationship with him or her for the sake of the children, I suggest you read *Forgiveness*, by Charles Stanley, and *Forgive and Forget: Healing the Hurts We Don't Deserve*, by Lewis B. Smedes.

According to Charles Stanley, forgiveness involves

three elements: injury, a debt resulting from the injury, and a cancellation of the debt. All three elements are essential if forgiveness is to take place. The person who has an unforgiving spirit is always the real loser, much more so than the one against whom the grudge is held. He says,

Forgiveness is liberating, but it is also sometimes painful. It is liberating because we are freed from the heavy load of guilt, bitterness, and anger we have harbored within. It is painful because it is difficult to have to face ourselves, God, and others with our failures. It seems easier to blame others and go on defending our position of being right, even though we continue to hurt. But the poison of an unforgiving spirit that permeates our entire lives, separating us from God and friends, can never be adequately defended. It is devastating to our spiritual and emotional well-being and to our physical health.[3]

Smedes says we forgive in four stages.[4] The first stage is hurt: when somebody causes you pain so deep and unfair that you cannot forget it. The next stage is hate: you cannot shake the memory of how much you were hurt, and you cannot wish your enemy well. You sometimes want the person who hurt you to suffer as much as you are suffering. The next stage is healing: you are given ''magic eyes'' to see the person who hurt you in a new light. Your memory is healed, you turn back the flow of pain, and you are free again. The last stage is coming together again. You invite the person who hurt you back into your life. If he or she comes honestly, love can move you both toward a new and healed relationship. This stage involves both parties. It depends on the person you forgive as much as it depends on you. Sometimes we have to forgive and be healed without the participation or knowledge of the other party. According to Smedes, forgiveness is love's toughest work, and love's biggest risk. But we have the power to free others—and ourselves—from undeserved guilt and pain. In his book he outlines steps to move from hurting and hating to healing and reconciliation.

Forgiving others is very difficult if you have not first forgiven yourself. Just as you must forgive your ex-spouse, you need to learn to unconditionally accept and forgive yourself. Remember that at every point in time you have done the best you could or knew how. Forgive yourself for any mistakes you made in the past, are making in the present, or will make in the future. If you didn't make mistakes, you wouldn't be human. No one would want to be around you because you would be too perfect, and people couldn't feel comfortable with you.

Also forgive yourself for the times when you have disciplined your children in haste or too severely or unjustly. Forgive yourself for the times when you weren't a good mother or good father or didn't spend time listening to your children. Forgive yourself for losing your temper and taking it out on your children. Forgive yourself for the bad decisions you made concerning your children. Forgive yourself for the divorce. You're really a great person, you know. Give yourself the same consideration you'd give a friend. Forgive yourself for all your human imperfections. You are a human being, not a god.

Forgiveness needs to take place not only between Mom and Dad and any third party who broke up the marriage, but also between the children and their parents. If parents don't set the example of forgiveness, the children are not likely to take the lead.

Children sometimes develop such strong resentments over the divorce that they remain with them for years or even throughout their lives. Children resent Mom and Dad breaking up the home, depriving them of an intact family. Children resent one parent taking away their right to see both parents every day and live in the same house.

Children also resent all the bad things one parent said about the other parent. And they resent being separated from their other siblings when Mom and Dad decide to split up the kids. Finally, kids frequently resent one or both parents for remarrying and complicating their lives with a blended family.

Teenagers resent the loss in their standard of living, which often forces Mom to go to work or take on extra jobs to survive financially. They also resent the stigma that is often attached to them in many areas of their lives, especially religious circles. And the affect of the divorce on their ability to trust and believe in lasting relationships is another source of resentment for teens.

Both children and teenagers resent one parent moving to another state so that visitation becomes infrequent, difficult, or impossible, as well as the times the parent was late in picking them up at the airport when they came to visit.

Although many parents assure children during the divorce, ''We are not divorcing you, only each other,'' unfortunately, children are frequently abandoned or gradually deserted, just as if they had in fact been divorced by the non-custodial parent. Children can never truly understand why their parents drop out of their lives; in order to feel good about themselves and go on with their lives, they, too, must learn to forgive. A beautiful example of forgiving one's parents is in a theme a sixteen-year-old girl wrote for an English class assignment. Her instructions were to write about a person either living or dead. Here is what she wrote:

This Man

This man has changed my life. This man has taught me what I want out of life and what I don't want. This man showed me right from wrong while helping me form my own opinions, values, and ideals. This man has no idea of the sort of impact he has had on my life. This man is not alive. This man is not dead. This man is my father.

As I think back over my childhood, he was never there to turn to for love, understanding, or even a hug. His cold-hearted attitude hurt, for I didn't know why he treated me as if I were nonexistent. In every attempt I made to make contact with him, I was turned away, only to become more confused and hurt, not being able to understand why a little girl's daddy did not want to see her. An obvious difference became apparent to me between my family and that of others as I saw the warmth and concern my friends' fathers showed toward them. I reveled in any extra attention given to me by these fathers and acquired a special love and admiration for them. The feeling of acceptance by a father was irreplaceable since it proved that I was not incapable of being loved as a daughter and it was possible that the problem existed within my father and not within me.

This man has not shown pride in my accomplishments, nor has he denied credit for them. This man has not encouraged me. This man has acted as if he could care less one way or the other about me. This man has not been involved in my life. This man is not dead. This man is not alive. This man is my father.

Without his help and without his guidance I have had academic success, I have formed high morals and have developed strong personality qualities which will take me far. His lack of interest in my future goals and aspirations has done nothing to restrain me. If anything, it has motivated me to show him up and prove that I can accomplish anything and I don't need his support to do it. Without him there for my first date and without him there for my first heartbreak, I still proudly survived. I learned to stand tall and set my sights high and not lower my standards, values, or morals for anyone. Without him I learned to remain firm in my faith and stick up for what I believe in. I learned what I want for my own children and what I don't want for them. Through his absent teaching by negation I have learned more from this man than anyone else I know.

This man has taught me how to laugh, love, and respect. This man has taught me the importance of friendships and the meaning of happiness. And most importantly he has taught me how to forgive. This man is not alive. This man is not dead. This man is my father . . . and I love him.[5]

The miracle of forgiveness does not come naturally. It comes slowly, but it's a sure sign of spiritual growth. Forgiveness is powered and propelled by love, but it involves a conscious decision of our wills.

Robert Muller said it so well with these words,

Decide to forgive, for resentment is negative, resentment is poisonous, resentment diminishes and devours the self. Be the first to forgive, to smile, and to take the first step, and you will see happiness bloom on the face of your human brother or sister. Be always the first; do not wait for others to forgive. For by forgiving you become the master of fate, the fashioner of life, the doer of miracles. To forgive is the highest, most beautiful form of love. In return you will receive untold peace and happiness. Only the brave know how to forgive. A coward never forgives. It is not in his nature.[6]

Forgiveness is necessary for healing a broken family. Eleven years ago I never thought it would be possible that my ex-husband and his wife could sit down at the table and enjoy a holiday dinner with my children and me. Now it has not only happened, but we are all comfortable together as friends who really care about each other's welfare. But most of all, we care about the welfare of the precious lives we share—our children.

Epilogue

Without question, divorce has a negative effect on everyone it touches. Some researchers predict that three out of every four children of broken marriages eventually suffer through divorces of their own. This vicious cycle is perhaps the greatest tragedy that divorce brings.

We believe it is possible to reverse this cycle, but to do this, parents must learn to look beyond their own grief and anger and keep paramount in their minds the devastating long-term emotional impact that divorce will have on their children's lives. Divorce may remedy some problems, but it often causes new problems that are more intolerable than the problems that caused the split. Our wish for our children and for your children is that they will do everything within their power to protect themselves and their children from the pain of divorce and not repeat the anguish of a broken home.

Only the miracle of forgiveness and reconciliation will prevent another generation of divorced kids.

Notes

1 HOW DIVORCE AFFECTS CHILDREN

1. Ken Magid and Walt Schreibman, *Divorce Is . . . A Kid's Coloring Book* (Gretna, LA: Pelican Publishing Co., 1980).
2. Barbara S. Cain, "Older Children and Divorce," *New York Times Magazine*, Feb. 18, 1990, 54.
3. John Bradshaw, *Bradshaw on: the Family* (Deerfield Beach, FL: Health Communications, Inc., 1988), 164. Reprinted with the permission of the publisher.
4. Barbara S. Cain, "Older Children and Divorce," *New York Times Magazine*, Feb. 18, 1990, 54.

2 DEATH OF A RELATIONSHIP

1. Frank D. Cox, *Human Intimacy: Marriage, the Family and Its Meaning*, 4th ed. (St. Paul, MN: West Publishing Company, 1987), 501.
2. Paul Bohannan, *Divorce and After* (Garden City, NJ: Doubleday, 1970).
3. Judith S. Wallerstein and Joan Berlin Kelly, *Surviving the Breakup* (New York: Basic Books, Inc., 1980).
4. Richard A. Gardner, M.D., *The Boys' and Girls' Book About Divorce* (New York: Bantam Books, 1985), 36.
5. Ibid.

3 MOURNING THE LOSS

1. Billy Graham, quoted in Lloyd Cory, *Quotable Quotations* (Wheaton, IL: Victor Books, 1985), 106.
2. Frank D. Cox, *Human Intimacy: Marriage, the Family and Its Meaning*, 4th ed. (St. Paul, MN: West Publishing Company, 1987), 506.

3. Ken Magid and Walt Schreibman, *Divorce Is . . . A Kid's Coloring Book* (Gretna, LA: Pelican Publishing Co., 1980).
4. "Over Two Million Children Are Latchkey Kids," *Marriage and Divorce Today*, Vol. 12, Number 30, Feb. 23, 1987. Published by Atcom Publishing, 2315 Broadway, New York, New York 10024.

4 THE ROAD TO RECOVERY

1. Abigail Trafford, *Crazy Time: Surviving Divorce* (New York: Harper and Row, 1982), 1.
2. Richard Flint, *Life Is a Maze*, (West Palm Beach, FL: Pendelton Lane Publishing, 1985), 52.
3. Gail Tabur, "Divorce Agreement Includes Loving Message to Children." *Arizona Republic*, Feb. 8, 1984, B3.

6 COMMON VISITATION MISTAKES

1. Judith S. Wallerstein and Joan Berlin Kelly, *Surviving the Breakup* (New York: Basic Books, Inc., 1980), 123.
2. Janice Katz, psychologist, *Marriage and Divorce Today*.
3. Richard A. Gardner, M.D., *The Parents' Book About Divorce* (New York: Doubleday & Company, Inc., 1977), 293.
4. Wallerstein and Kelly, 125.
5. Gardner, *The Parents' Book About Divorce*, 283.

7 GUIDELINES FOR VISITATION

1. Judith S. Wallerstein and Joan Berlin Kelly, *Surviving the Breakup* (New York: Basic Books, Inc., 1980), 123.

8 WHEN A CHILD HAS TO TRAVEL

1. Ann Landers, Creators Syndicate, *The Mesa Tribune*, Mesa, AZ, Nov. 2, 1987. Used by permission.

10 BETWEEN VISITS

1. George Newman, *101 Ways to Be a Long-Distance Super-Dad* (Mt. View, CA: Blossom Valley Press, 1981), 13.
2. Judith S. Wallerstein and Joan Berlin Kelly, *Surviving the Breakup* (New York: Basic Books, Inc., 1980), 215.
3. Richard A. Gardner, M.D., *The Parents' Book About Divorce* (New York: Doubleday & Company, Inc., 1977), 291.

11 COMMUNICATING WITH A HOSTILE EX-SPOUSE

1. Judith S. Wallerstein and Joan Berlin Kelly, *Surviving the Breakup* (New York: Basic Books, Inc., 1980), 125.
2. Richard A. Gardner, M.D., *The Parents' Book About Divorce* (New York: Doubleday & Company, Inc., 1977), 297.

3. Vance Packard, *Our Endangered Children, Growing Up in a Changing World* (Boston: Little, Brown & Co., 1983), 212.
4. Robert Eliot, M.D., and Dennis L. Breo, *Is It Worth Dying For?* (New York: Bantam Books, Inc., 1984), back cover.

12 COMMUNICATING WITH HOSTILE CHILDREN

1. Richard A. Gardner, M.D., *The Parents' Book About Divorce* (New York: Doubleday & Company, Inc., 1977), 287.
2. Ibid.
3. Fullerton, California, Police Department, and the California Department of Education. Quoted by Abigail Van Buren, UPI, *The Arizona Republic*, Feb. 12, 1988.
4. "Parental Divorce and Remarriage Seen as Leading Cause of Problems for Today's Teens," *Children and Teens Today*, Vol. 12, Number 11, Oct. 13, 1986.
5. Luke 23:34.
6. Thomas Gordon, *P.E.T. in Action* (Wyden Books, 1976).
7. Denis and Susan Waitley, "Listen to the Children," *Seeds of Greatness* (Old Tappan, NJ: Revell, 1983), 137.

13 DOES DIVORCE MEAN DISCIPLINE PROBLEMS?

1. Lucile Duberman, *The Reconstituted Family: A Study of Re-married Couples and Their Children* (Chicago: Nelson-Hall, 1975), 58.

15 PROTECTING AND NURTURING YOUR CHILD'S SELF-ESTEEM

1. Jim Fay, Foster W. Cline, M.D., and Don Shaw, *Parenting with Love and Logic* (Evergreen, CO: Cline-Fay Institute, 1984).

16 TEACHING CHILDREN TO BECOME SELF-SUFFICIENT

1. Spencer Johnson, M.D., and Donegan Johnson, *Value Tale Books* (La Jolla, CA: Value Communications, 1975).
2. Joy Berry, *You Can Survive Trauma!* (Danbury, CT: Grolier Enterprises Corp., 1985).

20 TEACHERS: FRIENDS OR FOES?

1. John Guidubald, "Why Children of Divorce Fare Poorly in School," *Marriage and Divorce Today*, Vol. 12, Number 11, Oct. 13, 1986.

21 A CHILD'S PERCEPTION OF DATING

1. Barbara S. Cain, "Older Children and Divorce," *New York Times Magazine*, Feb. 18, 1990, 54.

2. Eric Rofes, ed., *The Kids' Book of Divorce* (New York: Vintage Books, a division of Random House, 1982), 94–95.
3. *New Woman Presents Best Cartoons From New Woman*, Fort Worth, TX.: New Woman, Inc., 1979.

22 HIS, HERS, AND OURS . . . THE STEPFAMILY
1. "Children of Divorce," *Reader's Digest*, May 1980, 133.
2. Kathleen L. Kircher, *Marriage and Divorce Today*, Vol. 8, Number 27, Feb. 7, 1983.
3. Greta W. Stanton, *Marriage and Divorce Today*, Vol. 12, Number 25, Jan. 19, 1987.
4. Mary Kehle, *In the Middle: What to Do When Your Parents Divorce* (LaBelle, FL: Shaw Publishers, 1987).
5. Megan Rosenfeld, "Stepmothers: Image of Wickedness, Casualty of the Fractured Family," *Washington Post*, Feb. 3, 1985.
6. Linda Bird Francke, *Growing Up Divorced* (New York: Fawcett Books, 1983), 199.
7. Andre Brooks, "Step Kids: Divorce Leaves Void for Parent Left Behind," *Arizona Republic*, July 31, 1984, 810.

23 FORGIVENESS: THE ULTIMATE HEALER
1. Dag Hammarskjöld, quoted by Rhoda Thomas Tripp in *The International Thesaurus of Quotations* (New York: Harper & Row, 1970), 357:10.
2. Charles Stanley, *Forgiveness* (Nashville, TN: Thomas Nelson, 1987), 16.
3. Ibid.
4. Lewis B. Smedes, *Forgive and Forget: Healing the Hurts We Don't Deserve* (New York: Harper & Row, 1984), 18.
5. Natalie Estruth, Mesa, AZ, 1989.
6. Robert Muller, former Secretary General of the United Nations. Quoted by Abigail Van Buren, UPI, *The Arizona Republic*, International Forgiveness Week, 1990.

About the Authors

Laurene Johnson is a Certified Reality Therapist in private practice and is director of Successful Living After Divorce in Phoenix, Arizona. She is an internationally known specialist, lecturer, and seminar leader for divorced families and children of divorce programs. Laurene received her B.A. from the University of Missouri and her M.A. in counseling from Western International University. For eight years, she has been a counselor at the American Graduate School of International Management in Glendale Arizona. She is a member of the American Association of Counseling and Development and the National Speakers Association.

For the past twelve years, Laurene has been a divorced mother of two children: Cheri received an M.S. in mental health counseling from Western Washington University and Brad is a junior at Northern Arizona University. She wrote this book because she saw and experienced firsthand the enormous challenges all divorced parents must face.

For further information on seminars, workshops, or talks for teachers, churches, or organizations write to 888 E. Clinton, # 2096. Phoenix, Arizona 85020 or call (602) 971-9333.

Georglyn Rosenfeld is a free-lance writer living in Scottsdale, Arizona. She received her B.A. in business from Westmont College, her M.A. in business from San Jose State University, and has completed her course work for a doctorate in adult education at Arizona State University. For the past fifteen years she has coauthored books and tapes for numerous motivational speakers. She also teaches workshops for children of divorce.

Her personal experience includes being both a custodial and non-custodial parent, remarrying, and becoming a stepmother to two children. Rosenfeld's son, Nathan Estruth, is now a graduate student at Harvard University; and her daughter Natalie Estruth, attends Wheaton College.